WESTERN DESIGN

M. J. VAN DEVENTER ○ INTRODUCTION BY ELMO BACA

PUBLICATIONS INTERNATIONAL, LTD.

CONTRIBUTING WRITERS:

M.J. Van Deventer is director of publications for the National Cowboy Hall of Fame in Oklahoma City, Oklahoma, and a former reporter and editor for several newspapers in Texas and Oklahoma. Her freelance articles on interior design, art, and the West have appeared in *Better Homes and Gardens, Traditional Home, Southwest Art, Cowboy Country, American Cowboy,* and *Cowboys and Indians.*

Elmo Baca is director of the New Mexico Main Street Program in Santa Fe and holds a degree in architecture from Yale University. He is a historic-building preservationist and writer whose articles have appeared in *New Mexico Magazine* and *Southwest Art.* He has authored or contributed to books including *Santa Fe Design, Southwest Expressions,* and *Santa Fe Fantasy.*

PHOTO CREDITS:

Front cover: **R. GREG HURSLEY, INC.**

Back cover: **KIRK GITTINGS:** left; **CHUN Y. LAI/ESTO PHOTOGRAPHIC:** right; **ROGER WADE:** center.

LEE ANDERLITE/*Yippy Yi Yea* magazine: 197, 220; **RITTER ANTIK:** 240R, 254-255; **ARIZONA HISTORICAL SOCIETY LIBRARY:** 17; **ARTE DE MEXICO:** 240L; **ELMO BACA:** 31T, 32, 34, 262; **ELMO BACA/BERKELEY MILLS FURNITURE:** 120R, 252TR; **ELMO BACA/CASSANDRA LOHR, OLD WEST COLLECTION:** 30B; **ELMO BACA/MICHAEL MCDERMOTT:** 298TL; **ELMO BACA/SWEETWATER RANCH, CODY, WY:** 256-257, 258L, 259B, 260T; **JIM BARNABY/NEO COWBOY:** 30T; **BUFFALO BILL HISTORICAL CENTER, COLLECTION OF PAUL STOCK FOUNDATION:** 48B, 242-243, 245; **BUFFALO BILL HISTORICAL CENTER, U.S. DEPT. OF THE INTERIOR, FISH AND WILDLIFE SERVICE:** 44R, 244, 245R; **BERGER/CONSER ARCHITECTURAL PHOTOGRAPHY:** 249BL; **MARK BOISCLAIR/CCBC, INC.:** 175; **ROBERT BRANDES:** 306; **WILLIAM CLARK:** 9TR, 247B, 305TL&B; **COLORADO HISTORICAL SOCIETY:** 15B; **COOPER HEWITT, NATIONAL DESIGN MUSEUM, SMITHSONIAN INSTITUTION:** 62; **COVERT WORKSHOPS/TIM CARTER:** 246; **COVERT WORKSHOPS/ROBERT WEIGLEIN:** 248L, 249T&BR; **CRANDALL & CRANDALL PHOTOGRAPHY:** 10L, 75B, 88BL, 96BL, 146B, 210; **GREY CRAWFORD PHOTOGRAPHY:** 8T, 9C, 57, 222, 281L; **LYDIA CUTTER/CUTTER SMITH PHOTOGRAPHY:** 205; **D&R BRETZFELDER PHOTOGRAPHY:** 7T, 11BL; **MONTY DAVIS/LIVINGSTON FURNITURE DESIGN:** 261L, 266L; **JERRY ENGLAND/CUSTOM WESTERN FURNITURE:** 304, 305TC&TR; **ESTO PHOTOGRAPHIC:** 53L, 56TR & B, 60BL, 280R, 281T&R, 288, 307TL,BL&BR; **ESTO PHOTOGRAPHIC/PETER AARON:** 102T, 146T; **ESTO PHOTOGRAPHIC/MARK DARLEY:** 85, 98-99, 140-141, 161, 217; **ESTO PHOTOGRAPHIC/CHUN Y. LAI:** 38L, 58, 60T&BR, 64C, 66247R; **ESTO PHOTOGRAPHIC/SCHECTER LEE:** 12TL&TR, 13B, 14B; **JAMES FRANK PHOTOGRAPHY:** 36-37, 75T; **GIATI DESIGNS, INC.:** 297; **KIRK GITTINGS:** 5B, 22, 50, 83, 101, 103-105, 107, 109-113, 115, 120L, 143, 152-153, 158-159, 201, 213, 237, 266R, 292-293, 298B; **KIRK GITTINGS/CONSTRUCTION PROFESSIONALS:** 100R; **KIRK GITTINGS/SYNTAX:** 89-90, 108, 147, 150R, 155-156, 236, 241, 269; **DAVID GLOMB PHOTOGRAPHY:** 157, 195T, 206, 208-209, 274-277; **DAVID HALPERN:** 26; **HEDRICH BLESSING:** 21; **R. GREG HURSLEY, INC.:** 33, 114, 145, 202, 223; **INNER DESIGN/LINDA BEDELL:** 167, 174, 186, 200T; **JERRY JACKA:** 12C; **JERRY JACKA/HEARD MUSEUM:** 118T; **WILLIAM HENRY JACKSON/THE ALBUQUERQUE MUSEUM, DENVER PUBLIC LIBRARY COLLECTION:** 20; **BRIAN KELM/DICHOS CABINET:** 265L; **KERRICK JAMES:** 24B; **RALPH KYLLOE:** 64T&B; **L. & J.G. STICKLEY, INC.:** 250, 251L, 253BL; **PAUL E. LOVEN:** 10B; **RICHARD MAACK/LA CASITA:** 106TLC&TR; **WILLIAM MANNS:** 290-291; **ADOLF DEROY-MARK & ASSOC.:** 106BL&BR; **DAVID O. MARLOW:** 3, 6, 180, 221, 267, 285L, 289; **RON MCGEE/DICK KAPLAN/WILD WEST FURNITURE:** 285R; **DAVID MICHAEL MILLER ASSOC./CARLOS DOMENECH:** 211; **DAVID MICHAEL MILLER ASSOC./REDDIE HENDERSON/R&R IMAGES:** 188L; **HERMAN MILLER, INC.:** 268; **MONGERSON-WUNDERLICH:** 68C, 69, 239, 270L, 271B; **TERRENCE MOORE:** 203; **BOB MOORHOUSE:** 15T; **JOHN MORTENSEN/RAINBOW TRAIL:** 294TR; **TIM MURPHY/FOTO IMAGERY:** 170, 133R, 142, 168L; **MUSGRAVE & FRIENDS:** 94; **NATIONAL COWBOY HALL OF FAME:** 18, 286R, 302-303, 307TC; **NATIONAL COWBOY HALL OF FAME/ED MUNO:** 67; **NATIONAL UPHOLSTERING CO.:** 31BL, 48T, 264BR; **NEW WEST FURNITURE CO.:** 61; **NEW WEST FURNITURE CO./RON MAIER:** 294TL; **MARK NOHL**/*New Mexico Magazine:* 91; **OLSON/HEIDI A. DAVIS:** 294B; **OLSON/SUNDBERG ARCHITECTS:** 278, 282; **OLSON/SUNDBERG ARCHITECTS/MICHAEL JENSEN:** 279, 280L, 283; **OREGON HISTORICAL SOCIETY:** 27R; **GENE PEACH PHOTOGRAPHY:** 9TL, 31BR, 70, 78L; **PHILMONT MUSEUM, NM:** 97; **TIM STREET-PORTER:** 21TL, 23, 24T, 25, 29, 59, 72B, 102B, 125, 190B, 191T, 219T, 235, 251R, 263, 286L; **TIM STREET-PORTER/GREENE & GREENE:** 252B; **PROFILES WEST:** Brian Bailey: 14TR; Peggy Daly: 72T; Mark Gibson: 13T, 96TR; Tim Haske: 10R, 92T; Michael J. Howell: 79T, 87, 100L; Kingston Collection: 74; Phil Lauro: 76, 93, 95R; Bob Leroy: 8B, 96BR; Patricia Barry Levy: 7B, 79B, 88T, 106TL; Josh Mitchell: 28T; Todd Powell: 38R, 95L; Branson Reynolds: 51; Allen Russell: 75C, 80R, 86, 92B, 96TL; **ROBERT RECK PHOTOGRAPHY:** 11BR, 264L&TR, 265R, 270R, 272L; **RIKSHOTS PHOTOGRAPHY:** Diane Cole: 63; Rick Harrison: 248R; **JEREMY SAMUELSON:** 88BR, 118B, 123, 126, 129T, 137, 179, 189, 190T, 212, 214B, 215, 219B, 229, 253T; **SAN DIEGO HISTORICAL SOCIETY, PHOTOGRAPH COLLECTION:** 19; **ROGER SCHREIBER/WHITE GALLERY:** 300; **J. WILLIAM SHANK:** 27T&BL; 28B; **ALEXANDRA & SIDNEY SHELDON/PALM SPRINGS DESERT MUSEUM:** 252TL, 253BR; **STOCK IMAGERY, INC.:** Garry Adams: 106BLC; Jack Affleck: 81BL; N. Bilow: 80TL; R. Dawson: 5T, 82; Tom Dietrich: 4T; James Digby: 78R; Henryk T. Kaiser: 77; **SIEDE PREIS PHOTOGRAPHY:** 52; **PAM SINGLETON/IMAGE PHOTOGRAPHY:** 124, 127, 148-149, 150L, 151, 154, 160, 177, 187, 188R, 191B, 193-194, 195B, 204, 207; **DAVID STOECKLEIN PHOTOGRAPHY:** 21TR, 40, 42, 296; **STUDIO SEVEN PRODUCTIONS:** 273, 307TR; **SWEETWATER RANCH, CODY, WY:** 258R, 260B, 261R; **PHILIP THOMPSON:** 178, 214T; **CHRISTOPHER THOMSON IRONWORKS:** 287; **CHRISTOPHER THOMSON IRONWORKS/SUSAN LIVERMORE:** 298TR; **STEPHEN TRIMBLE:** 11TL, 14TL, 54, 56TL; **PETER VITALE:** 53R, 55, 200B, 247L, 271T; **ROGER WADE STUDIOS:** 35, 41, 43, 44L, 45-47, 49, 65, 71, 73, 84, 117, 119, 121, 128, 129B, 130, 131-132, 133L, 134-136, 138-139, 144, 162-166, 169, 171-173, 176, 181-185, 196, 198-199, 216, 218, 225-228, 230-234, 259T, 272R, 295, 299; **THE WITTE MUSEUM:** 68TL&BL; **WYOMING STATE MUSEUM:** 16, 39; **TERRY ZINN:** 4B, 68R, 301.

KEY:

Numbers indicate pages.

C—Center	TR—Top Right
TC—Top Center	BR—Bottom Right
T—Top	L—Left
B—Bottom	TL—Top Left
R—Right	BL—Bottom Left

CONTENTS

INTRODUCTION

The idea of an earthly paradise in the West has fascinated European thinkers and storytellers since the days of Plato. Medieval European literature is filled with tales of islands and kingdoms where unbelievable riches lay waiting for discovery. The fabled Seven Cities of Antilia were miraculously discovered by seven shipwrecked bishops who fled the Iberian peninsula during the Moorish conquest of the 8th century. These "Seven Cities of Gold" became an obsession with the great Portuguese and Spanish mariners of 500 years ago.

The discovery of the New World, with its exotic cultures, flora and fauna, and natural wonders, fulfilled the ancient dreams and prophecies. With the English and French exploration and colonization of portions of the Eastern

ABOVE: THE CALIFORNIA COASTLINE OF NORTH AMERICA WAS PRISTINE WHEN SPANISH GALLEONS FIRST REACHED IT IN 1542–43.

seaboard of North America and the Spanish conquest of the Southwest, a new Western paradise still loomed on the horizon of the American imagination.

The size and magnitude of the Western region of North America was unknown two centuries ago. Although the Spanish had explored and mapped their own territories and were familiar with the Grand Canyon and the golden coasts of California, such knowledge was zealously guarded. At the dawn of the 19th century, the Louisiana Purchase and the Lewis and Clark Expedition of 1804–05 tantalized many with dreams of riches and adventure.

The natural magnificence and grandeur of the West is familiar to all Americans through popular culture, but still only recently experienced first hand by many. The in-

ABOVE: WYOMING'S YELLOWSTONE NATIONAL PARK, CREATED BY AN ACT OF CONGRESS IN 1872.

ABOVE: ESTABLISHED AS A NATIONAL PARK IN 1929, THE MAJESTIC TETONS ARE NAMED FOR THE
TETON LAKOTA SIOUX, WHO CLAIMED THE WYOMING AND SOUTH DAKOTA COUNTRY
AS THEIR HOMELAND.

as Canyonlands or Monument Valley. Some places in the West have such power to inspire the human spirit that they are commonly recognized as sacred.

NATIVE AMERICANS

The people who lived in the West before the European cultures reached them lived frugally and resourcefully, regarding nature as a bountiful mother. The geography of the land determined cultural expressions and identity. In the Great Plains, people learned to hunt buffalo skillfully, drawing upon ancient knowledge of tracking animals and crafting of effective

credible adventures of explorers, trappers, pioneers, outlaws, and Native Americans have left indelible memories in the nation's psyche and helped shape the American character.

For many, the Great Plains resembled an inland sea, romantic and melancholy, yet dangerous and dramatic, filled with thundering herds of buffalo and menacing Indian warriors on horseback. Beyond the plains, a jagged chain of mountains erupted skyward, defying passage to both humans and beasts. In the south, the Spanish

called these mountains *Sangre de Cristo,* or Blood of Christ, for their reddish and purple moods at sunset. In the north, Yellowstone and Grand Teton aptly described country filled with wild rivers, sulphurous geysers, and crystalline lakes. Elsewhere, the majestic peaks were called the Rockies.

The West seems to be cast by a larger, grander mold. Brutal deserts like Death Valley can yield to soaring pine and fir forests. Entire landscapes of sculpted sandstone in peculiar shapes have become beloved national parks such

ABOVE: THIS PUEBLO *OLLA* OR WATER JAR,
IN THE SAN ILDEFONSO STYLE, IS ALMOST
A CENTURY OLD.

ABOVE: THE CLIFF PALACE AT MESA VERDE NATIONAL PARK IN COLORADO, BUILT BETWEEN 1000 AND 1200 A.D., IS A SUPERB EXAMPLE OF ANCIENT PUEBLO ARCHITECTURE. *OPPOSITE:* THE TRADITIONAL FORM OF SHELTER DEVELOPED BY THE GREAT PLAINS CULTURES WAS THE TEPEE. ORIGINALLY CRAFTED OF TANNED BUFFALO HIDES, TODAY'S TEPEES, LIKE THIS ONE NEAR ASPEN, COLORADO, ARE OFTEN MADE OF CANVAS.

dance and artistic expression, recognition and respect for the Great Spirit has been a common bond for Native Americans. Recent study of Native American folklore and oral tradition has yielded a rich source of spiritual philosophy that many feel resembles Zen Buddhist and Taoist beliefs of the Orient.

Native American design and artwork are intimately linked with spiritual association. The process of creating art is an exercise in prayer and worship, and the artist or craftsman usually follows a ritual form of prayer while creating. Many contemporary Western designers seek inspiration from

ABOVE: A WALL OF FLAT SANDSTONE ROCK AT CHACO CANYON NATIONAL PARK IN NEW MEXICO.

weapons. Southwestern cultures learned pottery and developed architecture made of sun-dried clay and log timbers. California and Pacific Northwest peoples learned to make boats and canoes and fished the bountiful waters for their livelihood. All Native American peoples were skillful traders who traveled to obtain the luxuries of neighboring tribes.

Tribal warfare and rivalries existed among native peoples before the Europeans, but rapidly escalated when horses were introduced by the Spanish after the 17th century. Enhanced mobility on horseback transformed most Indian cultures of the West, diminishing the fruits of agriculture and enhancing hunting and warfare.

Still, Native Americans espoused a philosophy and way of life founded on a belief in a Great Spirit that is the source and nourishment of all nature and humanity. Though worshiped by the tribes in many forms of ceremonial

ABOVE: THE FAVORITE HANDICRAFT OF
NOMADIC PLAINS INDIAN WOMEN WAS—AND
STILL IS—INTRICATE BEADWORK.

Native American design and emulate the Indian philosophy of life in art. Today, Native American-inspired designs in fashion, furniture, and homestyle are reaching unprecedented levels of popularity.

EUROPEAN INFLUENCES

Two astounding adventures led to the exploration and colonization of the Southwest by the Spanish. Hernan Cortes and about 200 loyal soldiers stole four Spanish galleons off the Florida coast in 1519 and sailed west seeking fortune. These men would ultimately conquer the mighty Aztec empire of central Mexico, plundering great temples and discovering exotic riches. In 1529, a small band of men led by Alvar Nuñez Cabeza de Vaca was shipwrecked off of the Texas coast near Galveston. The group's wanderings across Texas and southern New Mexico and stories of rich Indian tribes spurred an expedition in 1539 by Francisco Vasquez de Coronado to search for the legendary Seven Cities of Cíbola.

Coronado explored much of New Mexico, Arizona, Texas, and California, but found no gold. Among the civilized Pueblo people of the Rio Grande watershed, the Spanish discovered an indigenous American architecture. Not as substantial as the stone temples of the Aztecs or Mayans, these Pueblo houses and villages were constructed of sandstone and rough logs and were mortared with mud plaster. Stone masonry was plastered with mud to achieve a smooth, uniform appearance. The

ABOVE: BUILT BY THE SPANISH IN 1782 AS A MILITARY DETACHMENT, THE OLD GUARD HOUSE IN SANTA BARBARA, CALIFORNIA, LATER WELCOMED U.S. ARMY TROOPS UNDER FREMONT'S COMMAND IN 1846. IT WAS DRASTICALLY REHABILITATED ACCORDING TO THE MISSION REVIVAL TASTE OF THE 1920S.

ABOVE: THIS PORCH OPENING, OR *PORTAL,* IN TAOS, NEW MEXICO, IS GAILY PAINTED IN FOLK-ART STYLE.

villages were constructed to resemble the landscape of the mountains and mesas, rising in terraces to four or five stories. The Pueblo villages reminded the Spaniards of North African towns made of adobe, a Moorish word meaning "sun-dried brick."

While many Native American tribes of the West were seminomadic, some Indians had developed simple but effective architecture. The Mandans of North Dakota built large earth-and-timber lodges. The Chinooks and Nootkas of the Pacific Northwest constructed long houses of log timbers that could house several families. During the 18th century or earlier, the Plains tribes perfected their mobile lifestyle based on the tepee. Except for the Southwest, vast stretches of western North America remained free

ABOVE: A HISPANIC *SANTO* ILLUSTRATES SOUTHWESTERN RELIGIOUS FOLK ART. ISOLATED HISPANIC PIONEERS LEARNED TO CRAFT THEIR OWN VERSIONS OF CATHOLIC SAINTS.

ABOVE: LATILLAS AND *VIGAS* IN THE CEILING OF MISSION SOCORRO, EL PASO, TEXAS.

of European influence until the 19th century.

THE TAMING OF THE WEST

The legacy of Spain's golden age of exploration and colonization in North America, roughly 1540 to 1820, is still evident in the American Southwest. Spain developed a unique system of colonization for the harsh environment based on the mission-church complex and the *presidio,* or fort. Soldiers escorted brave missionary priests, mostly Franciscans or Jesuits, into dangerous and unknown Indian strongholds to begin the process of winning new converts to Catholicism. After missions were built at great human and material cost, *presidios* were built nearby, and civilian settlements, called *villas,* followed. Not all missions or *presidios* or *villas*

ABOVE: MISSION SAN CARLOS BORROMEO DE CARMELO WAS BUILT IN CARMEL, CALIFORNIA, IN THE LATE 18TH CENTURY.

survived the challenge of the Western frontier.

NEW MEXICO

After Coronado's disastrous exploration of the Southwest of 1539-42, the Spanish Crown resisted proposals to colonize the northern Mexican frontier. A series of *entradas,* or scouting entries, from 1550 to 1590 found little of value or interest to the Spanish viceroy in Mexico City. *Nuevo Mexico* was considered a poor and miserable territory. Still, undiscov-

ered lands lay to the north, and the Seven Cities of Gold were yet to be found. Spain could not afford for the English or French to encroach on the northern flank. In 1598, Don Juan de Onate was given a royal charter to establish a permanent colony in New Mexico.

After the initial Spanish settlement of San Gabriel floundered, the new plaza of the *villa* of Santa Fe was established by 1610. According to Spanish law, the sides of the plaza accommodated the needs of a church (religious), governor's palace or city hall (civic), *presidio* (military), and merchants (commerce). Many Spanish towns and cities in the Southwest, including major cities like Albuquerque, Tucson, and San Antonio, still bear traces of the original Spanish village-planning system. Santa Fe's classic plaza

ABOVE: BUILT FOR THE 1915 SAN DIEGO EXPOSITION, THE PRADO ART MUSEUM IS IN THE SPANISH COLONIAL STYLE.

ABOVE: BUILT IN 1917, THE MUSEUM OF FINE ARTS IN SANTA FE IS A HYBRID OF PUEBLO AND SPANISH COLONIAL STYLES.

boasts the original Governor's Palace, the oldest public building in America and now the Museum of New Mexico.

From its humble beginnings, Santa Fe struggled for survival, attracting determined Spanish pioneer families intent on making a new start with the promise of royal land grants. At first, the lack of rain water and good soil were more of a challenge than the resentful Pueblo Indians.

The new Spanish capital provided a base for missionary expe-

ditions to the Pueblo villages in the west, north, and south. The 17th century saw the construction of great mission churches at isolated pueblos such as Acoma and Zuni in western New Mexico. The construction of the New Mexico missions was a symbiosis of European architectural form, Pueblo labor, and decorative motifs, tempered by isolation, environment, and climate.

The Spanish innovation of adobe bricks in the Southwest enabled larger structures to be built. Houses were built in simple linear, L- or T-shaped plans or in a square surrounding a courtyard. Log *vigas* supported roofs and thatch-like ceilings constructed of branches laid in zig-zag fashion. Corner adobe fireplaces and outdoor ovens were crafted in a beehive oval form. Floors were hand-

ABOVE: THE MARTINEZ *HACIENDA* NEAR TAOS, NEW MEXICO, IS A TYPICAL FORTIFIED HOUSEHOLD FROM THE SPANISH COLONIAL ERA.

ABOVE: THIS NEVADA RAILROAD STATION IS IN THE CALIFORNIA MISSION REVIVAL STYLE.

packed earth, and adobe benches, *nichos,* or niches, and cupboards were often built into the walls of a home.

FURNISHINGS

The excruciating overland supply route from Mexico City to Santa Fe—the 1,500-mile *Camino Real*—severely limited importing any luxuries to New Mexico. New Mexican home furnishings were sparse and practical. Carpentry was taught to Indian apprentices, and a few trained *carpinteros* settled in the new colony.

Early New Mexican furniture of the Spanish Colonial era (1600–1821) is crudely carved, massive, and primitive, yet possessed of an authentic charm. Seating was provided by a priest's chair (a generous armchair owned by the clergy or nobility), simple armless side

chairs, or benches crafted for use in churches or at family gatherings, or *fandangos.* Cabinets were more ornamental, fashioned in Moorish and Spanish Provincial style. The chest was a simple wooden box, sometimes locked, sometimes on a specially crafted pedestal; it was used to store the family's most valuable possessions.

A great upright cupboard, the *trastero,* was developed by New Mexican carpenters for all-purpose storage. Often featuring panel

ABOVE: SAINT MICHAEL THE ARCHANGEL, SHOWN HERE IN THE BAROQUE COLONIAL STYLE, IS A FAVORITE SUBJECT OF SAINT MAKERS, OR *SANTEROS.*

ABOVE: THESE BEADED MOCCASINS WERE PROBABLY MADE AROUND 1890 BY THE NORTHERN CHEYENNE.

doors with decorative carvings or cutout designs, the *trastero* had drawers, shelves, or a combination of both. With the introduction of quality saws, tools, paints, tin, and other materials via the Santa Fe Trail in the 1820s, New Mexican furniture art was transformed. The *trastero* became the most ornamented and decorative piece of furniture in the New Mexican household, achieving an elevated status similar to the English and American Colonial highboy.

Spanish pioneers learned to create textiles in a distinctive style called Rio Grande weaving. The Spanish also taught the arts of weaving and silversmithing to the Navajo, who now produce rugs and jewelry of exceptional quality. Special artists and craftsmen called *santeros,* or saint makers, made religious icons out of carved

wood painted with natural pigments. Wooden statues and wall plaques of popular saints were treasured possessions of the Spanish Colonial home and are still considered an important interior-design element in the Southwest.

Pueblo and Navajo cultures of New Mexico and Arizona have survived the European and American occupation, retaining strong artistic and cultural traditions. The

ABOVE: THIS RUG FROM THE RESERVATION VILLAGE OF CRYSTAL EMPLOYS PLANT DYES TO ACHIEVE ITS SOFT, ELEGANT COLORING.

ABOVE: THIS TURN-OF-THE-CENTURY *SOMBRERO* IS TYPICAL OF HATS WORN BY MEXICAN *VAQUEROS,* OR WORKING COWBOYS.

Pueblo Indians are among the finest potters in the world, continuing an art tradition at least 1,000 years old. Navajo women create rugs and tapestries that are comparable in quality to Persian and other oriental examples. Both Pueblo pottery and Navajo weaving are fundamental decorative design objects in the West, at home in any interior or situation.

TEXAS, ARIZONA, AND CALIFORNIA

The successful Pueblo Revolt of 1680 caused the Spanish to abandon the New Mexico colony and retreat to El Paso. Many homes and churches were plundered during the 12-year interlude before Diego de Vargas peacefully reconquered Santa Fe in 1692.

ABOVE: SANTA FE'S OLDEST HOUSE INCORPORATES ROOMS AND WALLS OF A PREHISTORIC PUEBLO DWELLING. THE FOUNDATION MAY HAVE BEEN LAID IN THE 13TH CENTURY, BUT THE LOG *VIGAS* DATE FROM ABOUT 1750.

During the 18th century, the Spanish aggressively colonized the remainder of their northern frontier. In southern Arizona and northern Sonora, Mexico, Padre Eusebio Kino (1644–1711) explored and mapped a forbidding territory, establishing an impressive string of missions, including the beautiful "white dove of the desert," San Xavier del Bac, near Tucson.

Fearing incursions from the French on the eastern Texas frontier after 1715, Spanish authorities moved quickly to create missions and settlements. A *presidio* and mission built in 1718 at Bexar eventually developed into the village of San Antonio.

While the English were expanding on the eastern seaboard, Spain retained a firm hold on her northern colonies. In 1768, officials in Madrid received news of Russian fur traders moving south along the Pacific Coast from Alaska, and their attention was immediately focused on California. Between 1769 and 1823, largely under the remarkable leadership of Father Junipero Serra, 21 mis-

sions were established in California, many still preserved. Yet by 1821, Spain's power in North America was waning, and Mexico had won her freedom.

THE SPANISH LEGACY

The long Spanish dominance of the Southwest has had an enduring influence on Western design. Throughout the Southwest and parts of the West, adobe architecture is a beloved natural building expression, perfectly suited to the region's dry climate. Colonial homes in New Mexico, Texas, and Arizona were built of massive walls with few openings for effective defense. Doors and windows were covered with crude plank doors, sheets of mica, or animal hides. Roofs were simple log beams covered with organic branches, straw thatch, and mud. Spanish and Mexican roofs leaked prodigiously.

ABOVE: THE SINGLE-BITTED HAND AXE WAS WIDELY USED FROM 1800 UNTIL THE CIVIL WAR. THE BOWIE KNIFE, IF LEGITIMATE, DATES FROM 1845–1860.

ABOVE: TRADITIONALLY, ADOBE WALLS IN THE SOUTHWEST WERE PLASTERED WITH MUD, AS SEEN IN THIS SANTA FE PATIO.

In California, advanced technology and superior building materials allowed for the construction of homes with pitched roofs covered with clay tiles. Otherwise, California missions and homes were constructed of adobe brick.

California, Arizona, and Texas missions incorporated more baroque ornamentation than the earlier New Mexico missions. Carved stone *retablos* framed the front entrances of many missions. Domed bell towers, arcades, and courtyards integrated with lush,

flowering vegetation are common features of the California missions. In California, both the missions and larger ranches functioned as self-contained and self-sufficient complexes featuring vineyards, kilns, tanneries, granaries, and foundries.

COWBOY CULTURE

The introduction of Spanish livestock into the Southwest radically transformed the economy and lifestyle of all Western cultural groups. Spanish horses captured in New Mexico during the Pueblo

ABOVE: CHAPS WERE, AND STILL ARE, AS MUCH A FRIEND TO A COWBOY AS HIS HAT. THESE SHOTGUN-PATTERN LEATHER CHAPS DATE FROM AROUND 1895 TO 1910.

ABOVE: A PANOPLY OF COWBOY GEAR— SADDLE, SADDLEBAGS, BRIDLE, CURB BIT, SPURS, AND MAGUEY ROPE.

Revolt of 1680 rapidly proliferated among the nomadic Indian tribes of the West, who quickly became expert horsemen. Power shifted to the fearsome warriors on horseback, such as the Kiowas, Comanches, and Apaches.

Hardy Spanish breeds like the *churro* sheep and longhorn cattle, trained to roam free on the vast common pastures of central Spain, instantly adapted to conditions in the New World. Spanish horsemen and cattle breeders had already developed the arts of branding, roundup, and roping before arriving in the Americas, and even the contemporary cowboy fashions of big hat, boots, and chaps ultimately owe their design to Spanish prototypes.

By the early 19th century, California *vaqueros,* or cowboys, were raising enormous herds of

cattle and making great profits by selling hides to Boston shoemakers. The era of clipper ships facilitated early trade between the East Coast and California. In Texas, longhorn cattle expanded across the plains, enabling the rapid population of the Lone Star State. The roles of the Spanish *vaquero,* the Mexican *charro,* and the American cowboy in civilizing the West are intertwined and dynamic, still producing the unique Western cowboy design cherished around the world.

In 1850, the drama of the Western adventure was just un-

ABOVE: COWHANDS, CLAD IN CHAPS, BOOTS, AND COWBOY HATS, GATHER AT THE PITCHFORK RANCH IN GUTHRIE, TEXAS.

folding. Spanish cattle had multiplied in California and Texas during the early decades of the century. After the Mexican War, the first attempts to round up thousands of wild longhorns on the

Texas range and herd them to markets in the Midwest or the Far West succeeded. Spanish *caballeros* and Mexican *vaqueros* taught American cowboys the basics of ranching, and a new industry was born.

After the Civil War, a cash-poor Texas turned to its immediate and obvious resource—five million head of cattle roaming wild and free—for financial salvation. The great northern cattle drives, glamorized later by Hollywood, provided beef for the West's new settlers and the crews building the transcontinental railroads.

ABOVE: LACKING TIMBER, ROCKS, AND GOOD CLAY FOR BRICKS ON THE GREAT PLAINS, EARLY PIONEER FAMILIES TRIUMPHED OVER ADVERSITY BY BUILDING HOMES OUT OF PRAIRIE SOD. THE SOD HOMES WERE DARK, DAMP, AND FULL OF BUGS AND SNAKES, BUT THEY WERE CHEAP AND STURDY.

ABOVE: THIS PHOTOGRAPH, TAKEN BETWEEN 1890 AND 1905, SHOWS COWBOYS IN WYOMING
RELAXING AROUND THE CHUCK WAGON. ONE COWBOY, PROPPED UP AGAINST HIS BEDROLL, IS WRITING
A LETTER, PERHAPS TO FAMILY BACK HOME. ANOTHER SNATCHES A BISCUIT FROM THE CHUCK
WAGON'S FARE.

ABOVE: THE ROBBINS RANCH IN SOUTHEASTERN ARIZONA'S COCHISE COUNTY, SEEN HERE ABOUT 1900, IS A GOOD EXAMPLE OF ARIZONA'S TERRITORIAL RANCH ARCHITECTURE, WHICH COMBINED ADOBE CONSTRUCTION AND ANGLO-AMERICAN DETAILS, SUCH AS THE GENEROUS PORCH VERANDA.

Because of its early association with Spanish and Mexican cultures and later Indian, the cowboy culture of the West has always been a fascinating and dynamic expression of a unique culture tempered by necessity and survival. A cowboy's equipment was always crafted of tough denim, leather, wool, and rope to endure the long and punishing cattle drives. Big hats and leather chaps shed water, sun, and cactus needles. Today these same materials are fundamental to cowboy style but have been reinterpreted—and heavily glamorized—over time by Hollywood costume designers and high-fashion couturiers.

YANKEE SETTLERS

By 1820, many Americans were yearning for freedom, land, and adventure in the West. Unbelievable descriptions of the natural wonders of the West by explorers such as Lewis and Clark and Zebulon Pike proved irresistible. As the "near" western frontier of Kentucky and Ohio began to swarm with new pioneer families, many looked outward to New Mexico, California, and Oregon. Mexican independence from Spain in 1821 removed the final barrier to American westward expansion across the Mississippi River.

Wagon trains began the long overland voyage to Santa Fe and Texas immediately. Some New England merchants made the passage by ship to Monterey and never returned. Beginning with Stephen F. Austin's original 300 families who founded San Felipe de Austin in 1823, Texas was soon a haven for squatters, immigrants, and a flood of families seeking free land for homesteads.

The tidal wave of Yankee immigrants to Mexico's northern

ABOVE: THIS GOUACHE, *SUN'S LAST RAYS,* BY MICHAEL COLEMAN, SHOWS HOW THE ARTIST BLENDS
CONTEMPORARY SETTINGS WITH HISTORICAL SCENES. SAID ONE CRITIC, "WHEN (COLEMAN) INCLUDES
PLAINS INDIANS OR MOUNTAIN MEN, HE SUMMONS IMAGES FROM A ROMANTIC PAST."

frontier was sure to cause friction, which finally ignited armed confrontation. Texas fought her way free of Mexican control during the Texan War of Independence of 1835–36. The United States gained the rest of the Southwest from Mexico as the spoils of the Mexican War of 1846–48.

TERRITORIAL STYLE

New American settlers brought advanced technology, materials, and ideas to the Southwest. Common materials such as glass, paints, nails, tools, curtains, and wallpaper hauled over the Santa Fe Trail enhanced New Mexican adobe homes. After U.S. Army forts were built in New Mexico after 1850, a new architectural style was developed using adobe construction and classical Greek Revival ornamentation. The new Territorial style featured neat, square houses organized along a large, central hallway flanked by a pair of large rooms on either side. Trim white wooden columns in the classical Greek style formed impressive porches. Large shuttered windows and paneled doors marked a significant innovation in New Mexican home design. The Territorial style has remained popular in New Mexico to this day.

In California, the architecture of New England blended with the Spanish adobes to produce a hand-

some variation on New Mexico's Territorial style. Houses were expanded upward to two stories and crowned by a gable roof. Most prosperous homes featured a two-story columned porch or a cantilevered balcony on the second floor. Inside, the furnishings were a blend of English or American cabinetry and Mexican and oriental textiles and crafts.

Abundant trees in Texas provided great timbers for log cabins. Sometimes these cabins were plastered on the interior and decorated with applied stencil patterns. Great limestone quarries also provided abundant building materials, especially in isolated locations and remote ranches. Stone "ranch houses" and log cabins thus form the heart of Texas' vernacular architecture.

The news of the 1848 discovery of gold at Sutter's Fort, California, spread across the country slowly at first. A year later, an unprecedented frenzy of gold-crazed dreamers raced West over land and by ship, determined to unearth a promised motherlode. The California Gold Rush was only the first in a series of desperate searches for mineral wealth in the West. Between 1850 and 1870, gold

and silver would be found in Arizona, Colorado, Idaho, Nevada, and Montana.

Not all immigrants to the West were searching for precious metal. Fleeing persecution, more than 15,000 Mormons fled from Nauvoo, Illinois, to the Great Salt Lake region in 1846. Earlier, in 1843, the first wagon caravan of nearly 1,000 settlers successfully reached the Oregon country. Soon, a branch road led other adventurers across the Sierra Nevadas into California.

Astonishing timber forests near the Pacific Ocean in Oregon and California provided ready building material for homes. San Francisco, flush with wealth and new residents arriving daily, soared to cosmopolitan opulence overnight. The new architectural fashions imported from England—the so-called Victorian style—appeared in San Francisco at about the same time as New York. Only the Civil War could slow the construction of ornate Second Empire and Italianate mansions on the

ABOVE: THE WILD WEST WAS FINALLY TAMED WHEN RAILROADS JOINED THE FRONTIER TO STATES IN THE EAST FOLLOWING THE CIVIL WAR. CREWS OF IMMIGRANT LABORERS COMPLETED THE DIFFICULT, PAINSTAKING WORK.

ABOVE: LOST TO THE WRECKING BALL IN 1970, ALBUQUERQUE'S ALVARADO HOTEL REPRESENTED AN OUTSTANDING EXAMPLE OF THE CALIFORNIA MISSION REVIVAL STYLE, WHICH WAS POPULAR IN THE WEST AND SOUTHWEST IN THE FIRST THREE DECADES OF THE CENTURY. ALBUQUERQUE'S RAILROAD DEPOT BOASTED A "MODERN" INTERPRETATION OF THE CLASSIC MISSION BELL TOWER.

hills overlooking the city's impressive Golden Bay.

Oregon lacked the wealth, population, and outrageous vanity of San Francisco. Sober Christian families crafted simple wooden clapboard houses and log cabins in the heavily wooded Willamette River Valley. The Oregon and Washington territories grew slowly, numbering only 115,000 people by 1870. The completion of the Great Northern Railway from Minnesota to Puget Sound in 1893 hastened the metropolitan development of the Pacific Northwest.

THE VICTORIAN ERA

Most fans of Western culture consider the post-Civil War period to be the romantic "golden age" of

Above: Los Angeles's Heritage Square is now home to the Hale House, built about 1885 in the Queen Anne and Eastlake styles.

many other colorful minor characters with marquee names like "Black Jack," "One-Eye," or "Belle." While a few high-lifes dreamed of the gilded opulence of the era, as symbolized by Paris or San Francisco, in reality most Western pioneers struggled for survival under the harsh conditions of poverty, isolation, climate, and loneliness.

After railroad lines started criss-crossing the frontier in the 1870s, life began to change. Shipments of common luxuries such as fine clothing, textiles, and building materials offered Westerners a taste of Eastern elegance. Milled lumber in fancy Victorian gingerbread shapes, cast iron, bricks, and glass heralded a new

Above: This church in Oysterville, Washington, is an example of Victorian-era carpentry with Russian influence in the bell tower.

the wild frontier. After all, the three decades after 1865 saw the great migrations of settlers on the Santa Fe, Oregon, and California trails; the building of the transcontinental railroads; the ferocious Indian wars; the great cattle drives; and mining camps and boomtowns rising and perishing overnight.

These rambunctious years saw the creation of Western legends such as Sitting Bull, Wyatt Earp, Billy the Kid, Geronimo, Buffalo Bill, Annie Oakley, and

Above: The Greek Revival style, shown in this perfectly proportioned mansion, was the dominant house type between 1830 and 1850. After the Civil War, the style was transplanted to many Western cities.

architectural style in the West. Through builders' pattern books, prosperous merchants and families could construct up-to-date Italianate and Queen Anne storefronts, houses, and civic buildings.

Skilled carpenters and masons arrived daily in boomtowns. While many built "standard" Victorian house designs, others added personal flourishes and eccentricities. Competition among nouveau riche businessmen fueled the spirit of architectural fantasy

ABOVE: THE 1908 GAMBLE HOUSE IN PASADENA, CALIFORNIA, BUILT BY CHARLES AND HENRY GREENE, IS A MAGNIFICENT EXAMPLE OF THE CALIFORNIA BUNGALOW STYLE LARGELY DEVELOPED BY THE TWO BROTHERS. THE HOUSE EMPLOYS JAPANESE BUILDING AND JOINERY TECHNIQUES ALONG WITH THE WIDE, OVERHANGING EAVES TYPICAL OF JAPANESE CONSTRUCTION. *OPPOSITE:* SANTA FE'S ELDORADO HOTEL IS A CONTEMPORARY "POSTMODERN" VARIATION OF THE PUEBLO REVIVAL STYLE FIRST MADE POPULAR IN THE 1920S. DESIGNED BY MCHUGH, LLOYD, TRYK ARCHITECTS, THE ELDORADO IS AMONG THE TALLEST STRUCTURES IN SANTA FE.

original California architectural style based on the Spanish missions, many of which were in ruins.

California architects rallied to Loomis's challenge and began to reinterpret the planning and building concepts of the old missions. Graceful arcades, courtyards with fountains, curvilinear brick parapets, and clay-tile roofs were all emulated and formed anew on the West Coast.

The materials and palette of the new California Mission style contrasted sharply with the exu-

ABOVE: AN EXAMPLE OF THE GREENE BROTHERS' EXPRESSION OF THE CRAFTSMAN AESTHETIC IS THE IRWIN HOUSE, BUILT IN 1900 AND REMODELED IN 1906. THE INTERIOR BEARS A RESEMBLANCE TO FRANK LLOYD WRIGHT'S PRAIRIE-STYLE HOUSES.

that dominated some neighborhoods. In general, many Victorian homes and commercial buildings across the West were solidly built with quality materials and have survived waves of economic depression and revival. Many forgotten ghost towns reveal a glimpse of dreams, despair, and Victorian style. Other famous survivors like Telluride, Colorado and Cody, Wyoming still boast the regal

Italianate and Queen Anne architectural symbols of the Gilded Age of the West.

THE RISE OF THE NEW WEST

Even as many Western boomtowns were building avenues filled with ornate Victorian houses, the seeds of change were being sown in California. After 1885, writer Charles Loomis began a remarkable campaign to champion an

ABOVE: THE ARTS AND CRAFTS MOVEMENT, WHICH WAS POPULAR IN THE UNITED STATES FROM 1900 TO 1930, STRESSED STRAIGHTFORWARD DESIGN, QUALITY MATERIALS, AND NATURAL FINISHES.

ment based on the nobility and high standards of fine arts and crafts products arose in England and spread to the United States. The Arts and Crafts Movement championed hand craftsmanship, honest labor, simple and straightforward design, and the use of natural materials and finishes. In the West, the Arts and Crafts Movement became synonymous with the Mission style. Classic Mission furniture is large, massive, and crafted of dark-stained oak. Mission furniture rarely features any carving or ornamentation, and all structural elements are squarish and precisely cut.

In Pasadena, brothers Charles Sumner Greene and Henry Mather Greene began building houses inspired by the Arts and Crafts philosophy. These "craftsman bungalows" featured pitched

berant Victorian one. Multicolored "painted ladies" of wooden bric-a-brac gave way to the muted earth colors of Mission architecture. Fancy wooden millwork was replaced by adobe, brick, and stone. Proportions of buildings became lower, squatter, and more horizontal compared to the lean verticality of the Italianate style. Wrought iron, tilework, and plaster designs replaced lace, chintz, and floral excess.

The Mission style roared across the Southwest at the turn of the century, quickly adopted by major institutions such as the Santa Fe Railroad for depot buildings. The style found favor for Southwestern resort hotels like the famous Mission Inn in Riverside, California, and the Alvarado Hotel in Albuquerque. Mission-style houses even spread to some Midwestern cities. Thus, the Mission style became the first Western style to gain a national audience.

With the decline in Victoriana, a popular design move-

ABOVE: IN 1938 FRANK LLOYD WRIGHT BUILT FOR HIMSELF TALIESIN WEST, AN IDYLLIC DESERT RETREAT NEAR PHOENIX.

roofs with generous porches framed by simple, square columns. Craftsman details were evident in beautifully designed multiple windows, doorways, built-in bookshelves and cabinets, and great stone or brick fireplaces.

Publicized nationwide in magazines such as *House Beautiful, Good Housekeeping,* and *The Ladies' Home Journal,* bungalows caught the attention of families everywhere. Pattern books offered bungalow house plans for every budget, and bungalow "kits" with precut wooden elements could be purchased for a modest price. By 1930, the Southern California bungalow had become the favorite small-family house type in the United States.

A New Spanish Style

After 1900, the Mission style inspired California and other Western architects to experiment freely with the Spanish architectural heritage. Complex gothic arches and elaborately carved baroque plaster work of medieval Spain were married to Mission-style courtyards, verandas, and towers to create a new "Spanish Colonial Revival." Italian and French architectural details were also incorporated into the new Spanish or "Mediterranean" style, which became the symbol of California glamour. After 1920, the new Spanish-style mansions dotted the sparse hillsides of Hollywood and Beverly Hills. The "Hollywood" Spanish style of California was quickly transplanted by developers to Florida's Gold Coast communities—Hollywood, Coral Gables, the Palm Beaches, and Boca Raton.

The spirit of experimentation and reinvention of Spanish forms in the 1920s engulfed New Mexico as well. In Santa Fe, artists and other influential citizens led a well-organized effort to return to the timeless adobe architecture. The Pueblo Revival synthesized Pueblo Mission forms with contemporary needs of scale, comfort, and ornamentation. While adobe is still the material of choice in today's Pueblo Revival homes, concrete and steel often are adapted to Pueblo style for major buildings in the Southwest.

ABOVE: MONTECITO, CALIFORNIA, IS A SHOWCASE OF SPANISH ECLECTIC ARCHITECTURE, ALSO KNOWN AS MEDITERRANEAN. THE STYLE WAS FASHIONABLE IN CALIFORNIA RESORT COMMUNITIES SUCH AS HOLLYWOOD, PALM SPRINGS, AND SANTA BARBARA. ARCHITECT ADDISON MIZNER, ALSO KNOWN FOR HOMES THAT HE BUILT IN FLORIDA, WAS A MASTER OF BUILDINGS EVOCATIVE OF THE ALHAMBRA.

ABOVE: TULSA, OKLAHOMA, IS ONE OF THE GREATEST REPOSITORIES OF ART DECO DESIGN IN THE COUNTRY. THE DOWNTOWN PHILTOWER BUILDING EXEMPLIFIES THE GRANDEUR OF THIS STYLE.

THE METROPOLITAN WEST

The onslaught and ravages of the Great Depression forced many Americans to emigrate westward. Route 66, the nation's first transcontinental highway, was completed about 1926 and provided a new Western experience for American motorists. The promise of jobs and a new beginning attracted millions to California and the coastal and inland cities of San Francisco, Los Angeles, San Diego, San Jose, Sacramento, and Santa Barbara. World War II added economic stimulus as America's ship builders and airplane manufacturers located near the great ports of Seattle, Portland, Los Angeles, and San Diego.

A great wave of immigration to the West after World War II was fueled by cheap land, abundant jobs, and easy transportation and recreation. A new global architectural style inspired by modern machines and streamlined design, called Modernism or the International style, conquered the West as well. All historical traditions were rejected in favor of smooth, sleek, planar surfaces and manufactured materials such as chrome, casement windows, and glass block.

Emerging city skylines in frontier capitals like Denver, Salt Lake City, Dallas, Houston, El Paso, and Phoenix emulated the severe glass and steel towers of Chicago and New York. Earlier masonry high-rise buildings in the West boast Art Deco details or even regional touches like Pueblo Deco or Spanish flourishes. Today, with the recent economic ascendancy of the region on an international scale, Western cities boast homes, stores, and skyscrapers in Postmodern style that rival any example.

Modernism began to wane in the 1960s, and many have returned to traditional Western home styles. The preservation movement inspired many modern "homesteaders" to salvage wonderful Victorian mansions, crumbling adobe ranches, forgotten log cabins, and neglected bungalows in large and small communities across the West. Historic homes and small-town frontier life are

ABOVE: DURING THE GOLDEN AGE OF CINEMA IN THE 1920S AND '30S, LAVISH MOVIE PALACES WERE BUILT IN ALL THE MAJOR AMERICAN CITIES. DENVER'S MAYAN THEATRE IS AN ART DECO FANTASY CELEBRATING THE GREAT PRE-COLUMBIAN MEXICAN CULTURE. *BELOW:* THIS OFFICE TOWER IN SAN FRANCISCO BOASTS STYLIZED ART DECO WINDOW BALCONIES. DURING THE 1930S AND '40S, ARCHITECTURAL THEMES SUCH AS THE INTERNATIONAL AND ART DECO STYLES WERE IMMENSELY POPULAR.

ABOVE: THE FIRST PIONEER FAMILIES IN THE PACIFIC NORTHWEST ENCOUNTERED INCREDIBLE FORESTS OF PINE AND FIR TREES FROM WHICH THEY CRAFTED HOMES BUILT IN A COMBINATION OF RUSTIC AND LOG CABIN STYLES. THE IMPOSING OREGON CAVES CHATEAU, SEEN HERE IN THE 1930S, IS A QUINTESSENTIAL EXAMPLE OF THE RUSTIC STYLE.

ABOVE: THE NIGHT SKYLINE OF DOWNTOWN LOS ANGELES IS PERHAPS BEST KNOWN FOR THE GLITTERING CYLINDERS OF THE BONAVENTURE HOTEL IN THE CENTER, SURROUNDED BY MODERN CORPORATE OFFICE TOWERS.

enjoying a comeback and have never been more popular.

THE NEO-WEST

San Francisco and Santa Fe led the way in the preservation of Western architecture and culture. Santa Fe enacted a comprehensive downtown historic zone in 1957 that has protected and preserved many buildings. In 1963, developers turned the Ghirardelli chocolate factory on San Francisco's bay into a lively complex of shops, restaurants, and theaters. Soon, the city was engulfed in preservation fever.

New "yuppie" pioneers discovered the virtues of small mountain towns like Aspen, Durango, and Telluride, Colorado; Bisbee,

ABOVE: ON SAN FRANCISCO BAY, THE GHIRARDELLI CHOCOLATE FACTORY WAS REHABILITATED AND CONVERTED INTO A FESTIVAL MARKETPLACE IN 1963 AT A COST OF $14 MILLION.

Arizona; Cody, Wyoming; and Silver City, New Mexico. Combined with tourism and recreational sports like skiing, camping, and river rafting, a new economy for struggling small towns emerged slowly after 1975. Destination resort towns like Jackson Hole, Wyoming, and Taos, New Mexico, are the new boomtowns of the 1990s.

SANTA FE CHIC

Victorian style has been back in vogue in some parts of the West, as century-old storefronts and houses were restored. After

decades of sterile modern houses and office buildings, many Americans yearned for hand-crafted products, symbolic and ethnic designs, texture, and color. In the 1980s, American country style and Southwestern style captured the imagination of designers and homemakers seeking a new "primal" expression.

In many ways, the recent Santa Fe design boom resembled the Mission and Pueblo Revival of the 1920s. Native American arts such as Pueblo pottery, Navajo weaving and silver, Apache baskets, and Hopi kachina dolls provided plenty of fresh inspiration for popular cultural interpretation. Spanish Colonial crafts, especially New Mexico's primitive furniture traditions, have also been revived. Even the Mission style itself and related Spanish-style motifs, such as Spanish Provincial and Baroque furniture, are being transformed in the 1990s into a sophisticated Western Spanish style.

As demonstrated by talented artists across the country, Santa Fe and Southwestern design provides a broad range of themes, including Spanish, Mexican, Native American, Latin American, Territorial (classical), and Cowboy. The

ABOVE: THIS HOUSE IN SANTA FE ILLUSTRATES THE LATEST TREND IN SANTA FE DESIGN: IMPORTING NORTH AFRICAN AND MOROCCAN DECORATION INTO INTERIOR DESIGN AND EXTERIOR DETAILING TO BLEND WITH WHAT IS BASICALLY THE SOUTHWESTERN STYLE. A SET OF MOROCCAN DOORS, SET WITHIN AN IMPOSING ADOBE WALL, GREETS THE VISITOR.

juxtaposition of these traditions is what gives Santa Fe design its dynamic appeal.

THE NEW COWBOYS

The simultaneous success of Santa Fe design and popular movies such as *Dances with Wolves* have enhanced the appreciation and love of Western culture, touch-ing a deep chord within the nation's psyche. Revisionist films and books such as *Unforgiven* and *Lonesome Dove* have attempted to show the harsh reality and lifestyle of the West, but paradoxically the romance, glamour, and high style of "cowboys and Indians" are being celebrated instead in today's fashion and homestyle.

ABOVE: ARTIST AND FURNITURE DESIGNER JIM BARNABY OF BOZEMAN, MONTANA, EMPLOYS A FOLKSY AND SOMETIMES ECCENTRIC SENSE OF HUMOR IN HIS NEO-COWBOY COMPOSITIONS.

Wyoming's original Cody-style furniture, created and manufactured by Thomas Molesworth from the 1930s to the late 1970s, is now a major current in Western design. Over two dozen exceptional furniture makers in the Cody region are crafting dramatic sofas, chairs, and tables of burled fir, antlers, horns, leather, and Chimayo weavings. Carved silhouette figures of lonesome cowboys and bucking broncos capture the essence of the spectacular Yellowstone country.

Elsewhere, cowboy culture is enjoying a vigorous renaissance. Texas longhorns, rope, horseshoes, and barbed-wire designs are boldly decorating Southwestern cowboy furniture. At the other extreme, all kinds of leather, including cowhide, tanned leather, imported suedes, fringed leather, and stamped saddles, are being stretched over sofa and chair frames to create sumptuous seating perfectly at home in a Dallas penthouse or a Montana ranch home.

The Cowboy style of the 1990s has redesigned every facet of the frontier lifestyle, most significantly fashion. Multicolored cowboy boots, fancy fringed-leather jackets, full-flowing velvet skirts, Indian beaded buckskins, and re-creations of century-old army and frontier clothing allow anyone to experience a Western fantasy.

MISSION, TAOS, AND RUSTIC REVIVALS

The reemergence of Western design and culture after 1980 coincided perfectly with a playful spirit of revisiting and reinventing historical styles generally called Postmodernism. Besides the resurgence of major components of Western design, such as Spanish, Cowboy, and Victorian, other lesser-known themes have been rediscovered.

The sober and stately Mission style is acquiring new and graceful profiles, as innovative furniture designers are introducing stylistic influences from Japanese and Shaker traditions and from the old master himself, Frank Lloyd Wright. Whereas oak, leather, and brass hardware were among the few materials used in Mission furniture, today's Mission designers

ABOVE: CASSANDRA LOHR OF ASPEN HAS DESIGNED A STUNNING TEPEE WITH WESTERN AND NATIVE AMERICAN THEMES.

employ exotic hardwoods and a wide variety of upholstery materials to harmonize with Western interiors. A new bungalow revival is under way.

The famous art colony of Taos, New Mexico, has fostered a whimsical and colorful homestyle based on remarkable folk-art furniture. About 15 years ago, artists led by painter Jim Wagner began to decorate simple Spanish Colonial furniture with painted designs of dogs, deer, magpies, fish, chilies, and other typical flora and fauna of the Southwest. Charming and colorful *trasteros,* or cupboards, became the trademark of

ABOVE: CLASSIC TEXAS STYLE IS PRODUCED BY A LONGHORN STEER GRAZING NEAR A TRIO OF LONGHORN TABLES BY DESIGNER MILO MARKS OF MERIDIAN, TEXAS.

Taos Country style. Other variations of the Taos look include a technique that features thin, painted willow branches inlaid in dazzling patterns. Realistic Taos landscape scenes are also painted on fine cabinets.

The log cabin—that perennial Western favorite—is also making a huge comeback. The rustic allure of natural logs has been replaced by highly designed and engineered log palaces in all parts of the West, especially near jet-set havens like Jackson Hole and Aspen. Precision saws and finishing techniques allow for precise notching and fitting of logs and also for a variety of log sizes and di-

mensions to enhance the scale of a home. Synthetic materials help preserve the natural honey color of new logs.

Many Rocky Mountain craftsmen produce massive rustic furniture, often four-poster beds or dining tables, out of raw or salvaged forest wood. Combined with other rustic-looking Western products, such as plain Spanish Colonial chests and Cowboy longhorn furniture, the Rustic style can achieve a sophisticated harmony.

ABOVE: SANTA FE'S CHARM IS SYMBOLIZED BY A BLEACHED COW SKULL FLANKED BY HANGING CHILI *RISTRAS.* A GRACEFUL *CORBEL* COMPLETES THE PICTURE.

ABOVE: AN OVERSTUFFED CLUB CHAIR FROM THE NATIONAL UPHOLSTERY COMPANY EXPRESSES WESTERN DESIGN.

ABOVE: THE SPANISH COLONIAL PRIEST'S CHAIR OF NEW MEXICO IS A CLASSIC OF WESTERN DESIGN. TAOS FURNITURE'S VERSION OFFERS SIMPLE ORNAMENTATION AND MORTISE-AND-TENON JOINERY.

One of the newest trends in Western design is, ironically, the oldest. Native American art forms and design icons are being adapted for contemporary use. Spectacular lodgepole and canvas tepees are being furnished with elegant Western furniture and luxurious accessories. Pueblo and Navajo petroglyph symbols of humans, animals, cosmos, and spiritual beings called kachinas are crafted of steel or etched or carved into all types of furniture. The famous "ledger" paintings of the Plains Indians are inspiring hand-painted designs on Cody-style chairs and screens. Indian beadwork and buckskin are appearing regularly on high-fashion sofas, chairs, and pillows. Some Indian artists and craftsmen are attracted or being recruited to the rich bonanza of Western design. Native American home design is an exciting new development to watch.

THE APPEAL OF WESTERN DESIGN

Dismissed by many as an interesting and playful "fad" or curiosity for many years, Western design in the 1990s has finally matured and claimed its rightful place as a truly great and original American design tradition. Today, Western design is in the midst of a full-fledged renaissance, as all of its

ABOVE: A SIDEBOARD BY NEW WEST FURNITURE OF CODY, WYOMING, EMPLOYS THE TRADITIONAL MOLESWORTH DEVICES OF BURL STRUCTURAL COMPONENTS AND CUTOUT SILHOUETTE DESIGNS, HERE DRAMATICALLY CAPTURING AN ELK AND DEER IN A MOUNTAIN LANDSCAPE.

design expressions—architecture, art, interior design, fashion, and crafts—are being rediscovered and redefined for a new computer-age generation.

Even though the West was "won" over a century ago, it still offers a romantic and adventurous lifestyle and the promise of a new beginning. A booming Western economy is breathing new life into dozens of Rocky Mountain communities and creating metropolitan powerhouses in Albuquerque, El Paso, Phoenix, Salt Lake City, and Las Vegas.

Previously in the 20th century, revivals of Western design were short lived or regionally based (such as the Southwestern Mission style or the Cody or Molesworth furniture movement). Modernism's long influence inhibited scholarly and creative pursuit of historic design traditions. The current postmodern attitude of reinvention of the past has unleashed pent-up romanticism and experimentation with all Western art forms.

Beginning with the indigenous Native American art forms of the West, developed over at least a thousand years by Indian cultures such as the Pueblo of the South-

ABOVE: LOG HOMES ARE ENJOYING A SURGING POPULARITY IN THE WEST. THIS PAIR OF CABINS RETAINS THE BASIC RECTANGULAR GABLED FORM OF TRADITIONAL FRONTIER CABINS, BUT BOASTS EXQUISITE FENESTRATION.

west and Chinooks of the Northwest, Western design has evolved to represent a true antithesis and contrast to European aesthetics. Western design has sought to express a harmonious interpretation of man's relationship to nature, whereas European design has interpreted themes of man's transcendence over nature. Early Greek temples were sited on hilltops or other spectacular sites, and classical architecture was organized along principles of reason, order, proportion, and harmony. The intended composition of classical architecture was triumphant, a contrast of man's art over nature. Later, great Gothic cathedrals denied the natural order, as man's architecture and art forms were designed to inspire spiritual devotion

ABOVE: THE JAPANESE TANSU SIDEBOARD BY BERKELEY MILLS STUDIO IS ACCENTED WITH A CLASSIC CRAFTSMAN-STYLE LAMP MADE OF BRASS AND STAINED GLASS. *OPPOSITE:* THIS RESIDENCE IN McCALL, IDAHO, MAY BE DESCRIBED AS A POSTMODERN CABIN CHATEAU. THE IMPRESSIVE HOUSE FEATURES VICTORIAN-STYLE MASSING AND CROSS-GABLED ROOF SHAPES, WITH A COMPLEX INTERPLAY OF LOG-CONSTRUCTION TECHNIQUES.

still being celebrated on canvas, on film, and in furniture.

Western homes are colorful, boasting the trophies and products of the landscape—wood, hide, fur, and clay. Western design reflects the virtues of fantasy and adventure that lured the Europeans and Americans onward. As the Western landscape and its cultures, historical icons, and stories have been rediscovered by a new generation, the spell of Western romance and adventure works its magic anew. Western design offers perpetual themes for artists and craftsmen, and therefore its character is changing and dynamic rather than static and conservative.

As we approach a new century and millennium, the "Old West" of the United States, including its great cultures, cities, and designs, has finally achieved its promise and potential. The West has developed its own unique culture, born of an indigenous American style and tempered by European character, now an eternal influence on the lifestyles and art forms of the world.

In the end, it is the sacred, astonishing, unforgettable Western landscape that is the true legacy of Western design.

and awe. The human form, science, and intellectual invention were raised to new heights during the Renaissance. Humanism has been the legacy of Europe, and these design attitudes were largely imposed upon the New World by English, Spanish, French, and other European colonists.

The long isolation and pristine quality of the American West enabled nature to reign largely unspoiled by human culture. Native American architecture and dwellings in the West, such as log structures, tepees, and adobe villages, were organic and intended to blend in with and respect nature. These original Western architectural forms remain strong and vital elements of Western design.

Over time, with the exception of Victorian and modern buildings, European-American design has also succumbed to the powerful influence of the Western landscape. The incredible drama of the exploration and settling of the West is

THE ELEMENTS OF WESTERN DESIGN

A STYLE BORN OF THE LAND

Stand and face the awesome beauty of the Rocky Mountains, and sense the ruggedness of this land we so lovingly call "The American West." Gaze across the Grand Canyon and delight in the immense beauty of its bleached hues and painterly pastel colorations. Encounter the Grand Tetons and feel dwarfed by the majesty of these towering silhouettes that have captured the imagination of countless artists, writers, and photographers.

The West is a land so vast and so bold that we can only marvel at the extreme diversity of its geography. The landscape is formidable, beautiful, awe-inspiring, breathtaking, magical. With its expansive sky, magnificent cliffs, and sage-covered buttes, it is the only region of the country that seems big enough to hold the dreams that forged and continue to shape it. It is a place that gets in your bones, soaks into your spirit, and never lets go of you.

With all of the lore and legends, myths and realities, it was perhaps inevitable that the West would fashion its own style—one born of the land, spawned by the earth, inspired by simple elements, and hewn by hand from the humblest of materials.

ABOVE: THE QUAKING ASPEN IS ONE OF 15 SPECIES OF POPLARS NATIVE TO NORTH AMERICA. THE GROVE IS IN THE SAN JUAN MOUNTAINS OF SOUTHWEST COLORADO. *OPPOSITE:* A TYPICAL WESTERN SCENE FEATURES A RUSTIC LOG CABIN AMID FALL ASPENS, PEACEFULLY REFLECTED IN A LAKE NEAR TELLURIDE IN COLORADO'S ROCKY MOUNTAINS.

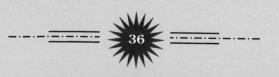

The West's early settlers were always mindful of the land and the way of life they left behind—a civilized, gentrified existence anomalous to the West. They traded a life of predictability and comfort for one fraught with danger and intrigue and blessed only by hope and promise.

These Western entrepreneurs had no choice but to rally their stamina, their sense of adventure, and above all their inventiveness to create from the land a functional design style. It is to their credit that the remnants of those first Western designs endure and prosper today.

Here, in this land of harshness and contrast, the elements of work, and occasional play, became the symbols of Western design. Sod from the earth became one family's dugout. The lodgepole-pine trees of the forest became another's log cabin.

Twigs, sticks, and roots became chairs and tables. Old wagon wheels were cleverly converted to tables. Cattle provided not only food but rawhide, leather, and suede for boots and jackets, saddles and chairs.

Nothing was wasted in these early Western designs. The longhorns of a steer or the antlers of a deer were transformed into table bases and candleholders. Native American blankets and pieced quilts became more than warm bed coverings; they brightened the walls of simple log cabins and adobe dwellings as pieces of art. Baskets, pottery, and wooden bowls were both utilitarian and decorative.

From such meager beginnings was born a design style that served our ancestors well and continues to captivate our imagination today.

ABOVE: GHOST TOWNS DOT THE LANDSCAPE OF THE WEST, SERVING AS VISUAL REMINDERS OF THE WESTERN WAY OF LIFE DURING PIONEER DAYS. MANY ARE POPULAR TOURIST ATTRACTIONS; OTHERS, LIKE NEW MEXICO'S SHAKESPEARE GHOST TOWN SHOWN HERE, ARE RELICS OF OUR ARCHITECTURAL HERITAGE. *ABOVE LEFT:* EARLY WESTERN FURNISHINGS WERE CRAFTED OF THE MOST HUMBLE MATERIALS—INCLUDING TWIGS AND STICKS, WHICH WERE USED TO CREATE THE PINE-AND-HICKORY PLANT STAND SHOWN HERE. THIS RUSTIC ACCESSORY WAS MADE SOMETIME DURING THE LATE 19TH OR EARLY 20TH CENTURY. *OPPOSITE:* BILLY CRAMER, SHOWN IN THIS 1899 PHOTO, WAS A ROUGH-AND-TOUGH BRONC RIDER, PERFORMING IN TURN-OF-THE-CENTURY RODEOS. RIDING MEAN BRONCS AND WIELDING A WICKED LARIAT, CRAMER CARVED OUT A RODEO COWBOY'S LIVING ON WYOMING'S RUGGED TERRAIN.

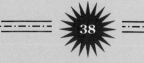

FROM HUMBLE TOOLS A STYLE IS BORN

A xes. Saws. Hammers. The crudest of small pen knives wrapped in their own sheaths. Nails were a luxury as the West was taking shape, prompting log cabins and furniture held together by careful dovetailing or mortise-and-tenon construction.

From such sparse materials, and from trees indigenous to the region, came rustic, functional homes and furnishings that have created our visual vocabulary of Western design.

There was simply no money for expensive tools, materials, and equipment. The spirit of "making do" prevailed. Homes and furnishings had to be spare, sturdy, and built to last. Many of these early tools and furnishings,

crafted out of sheer necessity by the town blacksmith, wood craftsman, and "whittler," survive today in Western museums. They are authentic remnants of our past, reminders of how our ancestors shaped and tamed their small parcel of the West, using whatever was at hand.

Today's designers and architects, respectful of hundred-year-old traditions in Western architecture, try to replicate—although with far more sophisticated tools and equipment—the rustic beauty of the old log cabins and adobe homes. Mortice-and-tenon construction is still used, as is dovetailing, but with materials now in abundance, the spirit of making do has given way to one of creativity in structure and design.

ABOVE: EARLY PIONEERS USED LOGS TO BUILD SMALL, SIMPLE HOUSES LONG BEFORE MILLED LUMBER WAS AVAILABLE. *OPPOSITE:* WOODEN CRISS-CROSS BEAMS NOT ONLY PROVIDE ARCHITECTURAL AND STRUCTURAL SUPPORT, BUT ALSO FORM A CATHEDRAL-STYLE LOOK IN THIS HOME BUILT BY TIMBERHOUSE IN HELENA, MONTANA.

WAGON WHEELS AND LODGEPOLE PINE

Lodgepole pine symbolizes sturdiness. The furnishings made from it reflect the rugged individualism that is so much a part of the West. Whether peeled and hewn by a craftsman's hand or ordered from a kit, lodgepole-pine furnishings and log-cabin homes typify the Western spirit.

With its knotholes, cracks, blemishes, rings, and beetle carvings, lodgepole pine continues to attract the craftsman's artistry. Its counterpart is burled wood, gnarled and knotted

pieces of timber that give even more meaning to the fine art of improvisation. Often, these burled roots are fashioned into braces, lamp bases, stump stools, chairs, tables, beds, or adorning finials.

Equally inventive are new uses for old wagon wheels. Long after the ruts they made on their path to the West disappeared, they have been revived as bases for dining tables, chandeliers, or holders for hanging baskets. Many still line fences, as borders, gates, or nostalgic decorations.

ABOVE: OLD WAGON WHEELS MAINTAIN THEIR FUNCTIONAL HERITAGE AS HISTORICAL REMNANTS, LINING FENCES AND BARNS OR SERVING AS TABLE BASES AND CHANDELIERS. *OPPOSITE:* MONTANA LOG HOMES BUILT THIS DWELLING IN STEAMBOAT SPRINGS, COLORADO. THE LOG DETAILING OF THE FRONT DECK IS COMPLEMENTED BY OVERSIZE TWIG CHAIRS AND A LOG END TABLE. PETUNIAS BLOOM ON THE SUN-DRENCHED DECK. NEARBY ASPENS PROVIDE SHADE AND THEIR RUSTLING LEAVES A SOOTHING MUSIC.

ABOVE

THE LOFT AREA OF THE GREAT ROOM IN THIS STEAMBOAT SPRINGS, COLORADO, HOME OVERLOOKS THE MAIN LIVING AREA. THE BALCONY IS LINED WITH LOG RAILINGS. THE CEILING SUPPORT BEAMS ARE IN THE RUSTIC STYLE, WITH NATURAL IMPERFECTIONS REVEALED IN THE ROUGHLY TEXTURED LOGS. NAVAJO RUGS ADD HISTORICAL INTEREST AND TEXTURAL SOFTNESS.

OPPOSITE

GUESTS AT THE KOOTENAI LODGE IN SWAN LAKE, MONTANA, CAN SIT BY THE WINDOW AND ENJOY A PLACID VIEW OF NATURE. THE OLD LODGEPOLE-PINE BENCH IS UPHOLSTERED FOR COMFORT, WITH FLORAL PILLOWS AND A LAMP SHADE ADDING A HINT OF THE VICTORIAN ERA.

BELOW

BURLED-WOOD FEET ANCHOR THIS LEATHER-AND-LOG LOVESEAT MADE BY THOMAS MOLESWORTH. LEATHER PIPING AND NAILHEAD STUDS ARE HIS TRADEMARKS. THE RED LOVESEAT WAS FEATURED IN A 1989 RETROSPECTIVE OF MOLESWORTH'S CONTRIBUTIONS TO WESTERN DESIGN, PRESENTED BY THE BUFFALO BILL HISTORICAL CENTER IN CODY, WYOMING. THE CENTER HAS THE MOST EXTENSIVE PERMANENT COLLECTION OF MOLESWORTH FURNISHINGS OF ANY WESTERN MUSEUM.

RAWHIDE, LEATHER, AND SUEDE

attle, buffalo, and horses have always led a double life—first as helpmate along the Western trails, then as warm fashion, furnishings, and tack. Nowhere but in the West would a buffalo come back to life as a mammoth overstuffed chair. Cattle and horses have long had a second life as hand-tooled saddles, saddlebags, rugs, upholstery, chaps, and all manner of wearable art.

Such elements of Western design now enjoy a renaissance of interest,

not only for utilitarian purposes, but as accessories, too. The leather chaps of a *vaquero* or an Indian's moccasins, quivers, or beaded leather dress now hang on walls, as beautiful as any Western painting.

Pelts line a stairway or grace a floor. Leather wraps a stair rail. Pillows and throws invite coziness and comfort. Strips of cow, horse, or antelope hide become chairs, woven as expertly as cane, lending that Wild West look perfect for any cowboy's corral.

ABOVE: NATIVE AMERICAN ARTIFACTS ADORN THIS LOG HOME IN KETCHUM, IDAHO. A BEADWORK SHIRT MOVES FROM THE MUSEUM CASE TO THE RESIDENTIAL WALL, WHILE OTHER VINTAGE BEADWORK PIECES DECORATE THE BENCH. *OPPOSITE:* COWBOYS AND INDIANS RESIDE HARMONIOUSLY IN THIS IDAHO HOME. IN THE DOWNSTAIRS ENTRANCE HALL, ORIENTAL RUGS CONTRAST THE CEILING *VIGAS,* WHILE A TURN-OF-THE-CENTURY HORN SOFA RESIDES HAPPILY BESIDE A NATIVE AMERICAN BASKET.

ABOVE

THIS SOFT, BROWN-LEATHER SOFA INVITES REST AND RELAXATION. ITS GENTLY SCALLOPED BACK ADDS AN ARCHITECTURAL DETAIL TO THE PIECE, WHILE THE NAILHEAD TRIM MARKS ITS CHARACTER AS A TRUE WESTERN FURNISHING. A SUEDE PILLOW PAINTED WITH A NATIVE AMERICAN MOTIF AND TRIMMED IN LEATHER FRINGE ACCENTS THE SOFA.

LEFT

THOMAS MOLESWORTH USED BLACK AND RED LEATHER AND WOOD TO CREATE THIS CHAIR, WHICH INCLUDES A CHIMAYO WOVEN DESIGN ON THE BACK CUSHION. MOLESWORTH OFTEN WORKED SUCH NATIVE AMERICAN MOTIFS INTO HIS DESIGNS. THE CHAIR WAS AMONG ARTIFACTS INCLUDED IN A 1989 EXHIBITION AT THE BUFFALO BILL HISTORICAL CENTER IN CODY, WYOMING.

OPPOSITE

THE ACCESSORIES THAT DECORATE THIS VICTOR, MONTANA, HOME SHOW THE INFLUENCE OF RUGGED OUTDOOR SPORTS—SADDLES AND CHAPS FOR RIDING HORSES, GUNS FOR HUNTING, CREELS AND VESTS FOR FISHING.

WESTERN WEAVINGS AND QUILTS

mong the oldest of Western-design art forms, Native American weavings have long been more than a symbol of warmth. With their colorful stripes, geometrics, rectangles, crosses, arrows, diamonds, and pictorials, they also have been a means of barter.

The idea of trade was never lost on the Navajos or the Hopis. They responded quickly to traders' ideas, adapting their designs to please tourists eager to add a touch of the

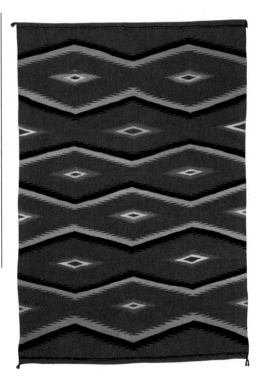

West to their own homes. Now, these creative tapestries are collectors' items, whether in their original state or in new forms.

Quilts are as important in Western design as Native American weavings. Nothing expresses the heritage of the West more than quilts or rag rugs, lovingly stitched or braided by an ancestor's hand. Pieced together from scraps of frontier materials, these storytelling quilts and rugs reflect homespun motifs, creating a visual mosaic of life in the early West.

ABOVE: A NAVAJO CHIEF'S WOVEN BLANKET REVEALS A TRADITIONAL PATTERN. *OPPOSITE:* A NAVAJO WOMAN WEAVES RUGS IN HER HOGAN ON A RESERVATION IN MONUMENT VALLEY ON THE ARIZONA-UTAH BORDER. SHE WORKS IN THE TRADITIONAL MANNER, ACHIEVING BRILLIANT COLORS USING ONLY PLANT DYES.

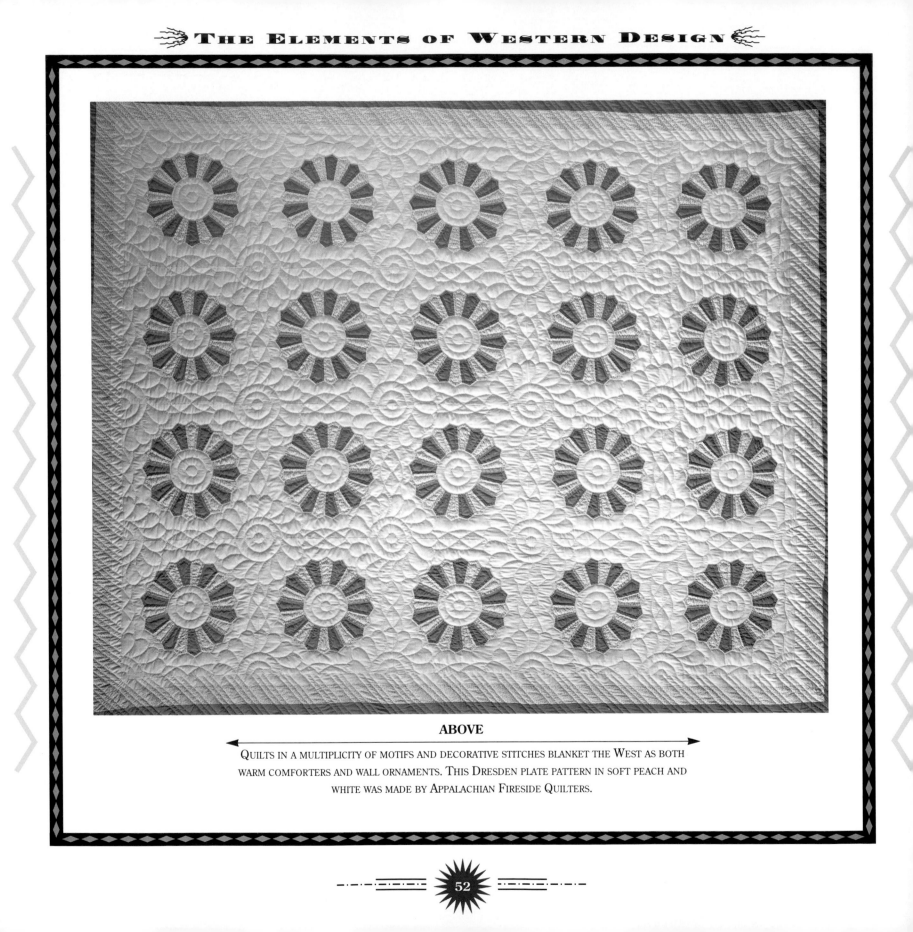

ABOVE

QUILTS IN A MULTIPLICITY OF MOTIFS AND DECORATIVE STITCHES BLANKET THE WEST AS BOTH
WARM COMFORTERS AND WALL ORNAMENTS. THIS DRESDEN PLATE PATTERN IN SOFT PEACH AND
WHITE WAS MADE BY APPALACHIAN FIRESIDE QUILTERS.

ABOVE

IVORY WOOL SERVES AS A BACKGROUND FOR
THIS BRILLIANTLY COLORED NATIVE AMERICAN
DESIGN. TYPICAL COLORS OF RED, BLACK, GRAY,
AND TURQUOISE WERE USED FOR WEAVING THE
DESIGN ON THIS COAT, WHICH IS NOW A HIGHLY
PRIZED WESTERN FASHION HEIRLOOM.

ABOVE

DESIGNER CHRIS O'CONNELL USED A WOVEN BRUNSCHWIG & FILS FABRIC IN A NATIVE
AMERICAN MOTIF TO UPHOLSTER AN ARMLESS CONTEMPORARY CHAIR. OTHER DESIGN ACCESSORIES
INCLUDE A DRUM TABLE TOPPED BY A NATIVE AMERICAN BOWL AND WOVEN BLANKETS THAT SERVE
AS COZY SOFA THROWS. PHOTOGRAPHS OF PUEBLO LADDERS BECOME ART FOR THE WALLS, AS DOES
A BEADED CRADLE BOARD.

BASKETS, POTTERY, AND WOODEN BOWLS

A rising from purely functional beginnings, baskets, pottery, and wooden bowls shaped from the environment are now museum pieces and collectibles. Drawing from the rawness of the land, these vessels were molded into pieces of exquisite beauty.

Native American baskets predate pottery and, like Native American weavings, also were a form of currency. Both pottery and baskets became a status symbol in the 1930s, signifying that one was rich enough to have traveled West. Baskets—such intricate beauties—are judged by their weaving, contrasting colors, or unique designs.

Pottery is judged by its glazes. Some contemporary versions are sculpted by hand and adorned with logs, stones, strips of leather and rope, feathers, fetishes, and quills.

Wooden bowls are like country cousins. Often fashioned into primitive shapes, they have held everything from corn to millet. Today, these utilitarian pieces are collected by those who envision themselves as custodians of the past.

LEFT: THE ARTIST BLUE CORN OF THE SAN ILDEFONSO PUEBLO IN NEW MEXICO CREATED THIS POLYCHROME BOWL USING AN UNUSUAL COLOR THEME IN SAND, PEACH, ECRU, AND PURPLE. THE BOWL BELONGS TO THE KATHERINE H. RUST CHILDREN'S COLLECTION AT THE MUDD-CARR GALLERY IN SANTA FE, NEW MEXICO.

OPPOSITE: CHRIS O'CONNELL DESIGNED THE INTERIORS FOR THIS HOME IN SANTA FE AND CREATED DISPLAY SPACES FOR THE FAMILY'S SOUTHWEST COLLECTION. HEIRLOOM EDWARD CURTIS PHOTOGRAPHS, NATIVE AMERICAN POTTERY, STONE CROSSES FROM OLD MISSIONS, SILVER SPOONS, AND PEWTER CANDLESTICKS GRACE THE SHELVES. A SMALL BOWL HOLDS CORN STALKS. A WOODEN PLANTER ON THE TOP SHELF ECHOES THE WOOD FRAMES AROUND THE CURTIS PHOTOGRAPHS.

OPPOSITE

NATIVE AMERICAN POTTERY TRADITIONALLY EMPLOYS A VARIETY OF PATTERNS AND DESIGNS USING RECTANGLES, SQUARES, TRIANGLES, AND ZIGZAGS. AN INDIAN WARRIOR, COMPLETE WITH DECORATIVE SHIELD AND ARROW, MARCHES ACROSS THIS BOWL IN PURSUIT OF HIS MYTHICAL FOE. PLAINS INDIAN MOTIFS FREQUENTLY FEATURED A BATTLE THEME.

ABOVE

LEFT: JOSEPHINE HARRISON OF THE ARIZONA YAVAPAI TRIBE WOVE THIS DESIGN, CIRCA 1965. *RIGHT:* THIS COILED BASKET EMPLOYS TECHNIQUES DEVELOPED BY THE HOPIS, ONE OF THE FOREMOST BASKET-MAKING GROUPS IN NORTH AMERICA, ACCORDING TO AUTHOR AND HISTORIAN ANDREW HUNTER WHITEFORD. THIS LIDDED BASKET REVEALS A SUBTLE BLEND OF NEUTRAL COLORATIONS.

RIGHT

COILED BASKETS LIKE THESE REVEAL THE TIGHT WEAVING OF NATIVE AMERICAN BASKET MAKERS. COILING TECHNIQUES VARIED FROM TRIBE TO TRIBE AND PUEBLO TO PUEBLO, BUT THE RESULT WAS ALWAYS A BASKET THAT WAS BOTH BEAUTIFUL AND FUNCTIONAL.

PAINTED FURNITURE

Painted furniture has always enhanced the interior landscape of Western design. Wedgewood, navy, turquoise, bucolic green, and turkey red were favorite colors brightening humble primitive pine and cypress wood. No respecter of use, dry sinks, *trasteros,* troughs, mirrors—all were splashed with color.

Nowhere is the custom of painted furniture more prevalent than in those Hispanic painted chests and chairs, *santos* and folk art accessories, replete with ethnic, religious, and cultural symbols. Antique examples of painted furniture, of course, have acquired the patina of age, having lost much of their

original brightness. They are still valued, however, and displayed prominently in the Western home.

Western furniture makers followed in the Hispanic tradition, painting Western scenes on all sorts of furniture. When shipped East for summer retreats or hunting lodges, these wildlife and cowboys-and-Indians scenes furthered the country's fascination with the West. Today, Native American and cowboy folk-art scenes continue to give Western furnishings a sense of humor, showing that Western design, for all its ruggedness and larger-than-life allure, never takes itself *too* seriously.

ABOVE: EARLY-DAY CUPBOARDS IN THE WEST WERE BUILT ALONG SIMPLE LINES AND FASHIONED OF THE CRUDEST MATERIALS. *OPPOSITE:* THIS SANTA FE, NEW MEXICO, HOME DISPLAYS AN ECLECTIC MASTERY AND FLAIR IN ITS INTERIOR FURNISHINGS, JUXTAPOSING A FOLK-PAINTED ARMOIRE AND A CONTEMPORARY ARMCHAIR AND OTTOMAN UPHOLSTERED IN NOUVEAU SANTA FE FABRIC.

LEFT

PINE CHESTS WERE USED IN THE 19TH CENTURY TO HOLD ALL KINDS OF TREASURES—FUNCTIONAL AS WELL AS DECORATIVE. THE TWO PICTURED HERE ARE EXAMPLES OF UNUSUAL FINISHING TREATMENTS. THE LARGER CHEST IS SPONGED TO CREATE A MOTTLED FINISH. THE SMALLER CHEST, COMPLETE WITH METAL LOCK AND HINGE, HAS BEEN PAINTED IN A WAVING-GRAIN DESIGN.

BELOW

THESE BENCHES IN GRADUATED SIZES REFLECT THE SIMPLICITY OF EARLY WESTERN FURNISHINGS. FASHIONED OF HUMBLE MATERIALS, THEIR MOST DECORATIVE ELEMENTS ARE THE SMALL SCALLOPS THAT FLANK THE EDGES AND THE ARCHED CUTOUTS OF THE LEGS. PAINT—TYPICALLY BLUE, RED, AND MUSTARD COLORS—OFTEN SERVED AS THE FINISHING TOUCH.

BELOW

DROP-LEAF TABLES LIKE THIS ONE ARE STILL FREQUENTLY FOUND IN WESTERN HOMES. WHETHER PAINTED BLUE, LEFT IN THEIR ORIGINAL STATE, OR VARNISHED TO A HIGH GLOSS, THEY REVEAL THE SIMPLICITY OF FURNISHINGS. THE DROP LEAVES MADE THESE TABLES DO DOUBLE DUTY— EITHER AS A SIDEBOARD OR AS A DINING TABLE FOR COMPANY.

ARTIST ALAN MILLS'S DYNAMIC ILLUSTRATION OF A CALF ROPING ON THE OPEN RANGE GRACES A CABINET BY NEW WEST FURNITURE OF CODY. THE CABINET COMBINES LODGEPOLE PINE AND BURL; DRAWER PULLS ARE OF ANTLER.

ABOVE

NEW WEST FURNITURE IS AMONG THE MOST INNOVATIVE OF CONTEMPORARY CODY, WYOMING, FURNITURE MAKERS, AS AMPLY DEMONSTRATED IN THIS PAINTED CABINET FEATURING THE ART OF LANA PERATTI.

AS THE TWIG IS BENT

From such mundane materials as twigs and sticks, roots and bark, logs and tree stumps, nature yielded a mother lode of Western design. Sometimes whimsical, occasionally strange, these rustic, functional pieces are another example of pioneers' ingenious use of humble materials.

Pioneer furnishings were created from indigenous woods—the Midwest's hickory, the Southwest's scrub pine, the South's cypress and laurel, the Northwest's lodgepole pine. These furnishings evoke that Western spirit of

independence, humor, and self-reliance. They were, and are, the work of craftsmen who take pride in making furnishings that remind us of nature's simplicity.

Originally designed to cater to those who frequented dude ranches and lodges, twig and root furniture is now considered classic folk art. Even the plastics and aluminum of the 1950s could not eclipse the timeless, simple beauty these pieces express. Today, these bent twigs enjoy a new growth of interest in the most sophisticated of settings.

ABOVE: THIS ROCKING CHAIR, CIRCA 1920, MAKES IMAGINATIVE USE OF BURLED ROOTS AND TWIGS BENT INTO HALF MOONS. IT BELONGS TO NEW YORK'S COOPER HEWITT MUSEUM. *OPPOSITE:* DIANE COLE, OWNER OF RUSTIC FURNITURE IN BOZEMAN, MONTANA, CREATED THE FURNISHINGS FOR THIS LOG-CABIN PORCH. A BENT WILLOW SETTEE RESTS COMFORTABLY NEXT TO A TWIG TABLE AND AN ADIRONDACK BENCH. A WICKER BASKET HOLDS COLORFUL PILLOWS.

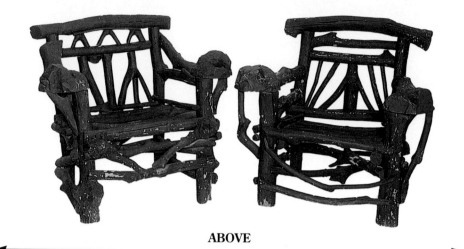

ABOVE

Twig furniture, including chairs, rockers, and settees, originated around the turn of the century and was made on the East Coast and in the Midwest, according to photographer Ralph Kylloe. Some of the best were made by the Amish in Indiana, Ohio, and Pennsylvania.

BELOW

These armchairs and magazine rack, built of rhododendron, were probably made in Asheville, North Carolina, around 1920.

OPPOSITE

The upstairs loft of this residence in Bozeman, Montana, which was built by Big Timberworks, is a perfect sportsman's hideaway. Snowshoes, a fisherman's vest, hiking boots, and a rifle are appropriate decorative accents for this room that could double as an office. The twig rocking chair with a woven leather seat is a perfect place for spending idle hours. Woven rugs and hides dress the floor.

ABOVE

Pine and birch bark combine to create an unusual plant stand that would feel right at home in the West. The shape of the legs and the floral pattern worked in wood subtly reflect Islamic and Mediterranean design influences, revealing the strong melting-pot flavor of Western design.

THOSE TEXAS LONGHORNS

Nothing is spared in Western design, and the longhorn steer is a classic example of ingenuity. Cowhide covers sofas and chairs, while hooves and horns become legs, giving cattle a rebirth few outside the West could have imagined.

Although horn furniture had a European birthright, credit goes to Texan Wenzel Friedrich for creating a unique style in the 1880s that is now being revived. Like Texas, horn furnishings are larger than life.

No hunting lodge was complete without a chandelier of elk or deer antlers, candleholders from hooves, or the stuffed head of a moose, deer, or bighorn sheep adorning the fireplace mantel like a symbolic sentinel of the West. Every Western aficionado worth his spurs must feature a bleached skull and fur pelts in his decor.

And for some Western folks, their car just wouldn't be the same without a longhorn hood ornament!

ABOVE: WESTERN HORNS MEET VICTORIAN VELVET IN THIS CHAIR BY TEDDY AND MILO MARKS OF MERIDIAN, TEXAS. *OPPOSITE:* THIS DRAMATIC AND ACTUALLY QUITE COMFORTABLE ELKHORN CHAIR, MADE ABOUT 1890, BELONGS TO THE NATIONAL COWBOY HALL OF FAME'S PERMANENT COLLECTION.

ABOVE

TEXAS CRAFTSMAN WENZEL FRIEDRICH BUILT FURNITURE AND ACCESSORIES FROM STEER HORNS. THIS FLOWER STAND HAS 36 HORNS AND A TOP WITH STAR INLAYS.

BELOW

CRAFTED IN THE LATE 1800S, THIS SPRING ROCKER BY WENZEL FRIEDRICH USES TWO DOZEN HORNS. THE BACK AND SEAT ARE COVERED WITH JAGUAR PELT.

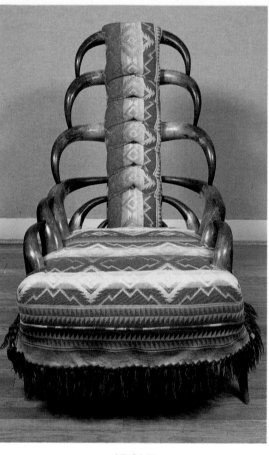

ABOVE

HORNS ARE ARRANGED IN GRADUATED FASHION TO CREATE THIS UNUSUAL VINTAGE CHAIR. THE SEAT AND TUFTED BACK ARE COVERED WITH A COTTON CAMP BLANKET. THE CHAIR, FEATURED IN THE MONGERSON-WUNDERLICH COLLECTION, WAS MADE AROUND 1930.

BELOW

A 1993 TRIP TO THE GRAND TETONS AND YELLOWSTONE NATIONAL PARK INSPIRED PHOTOGRAPHER TERRY ZINN TO BECOME A WESTERN CRAFTSMAN. HE DESIGNED THIS CANDLEHOLDER, USING NATURALLY SHED MULE-DEER ANTLERS PURCHASED IN AN ANTIQUE SHOP IN CODY, WYOMING.

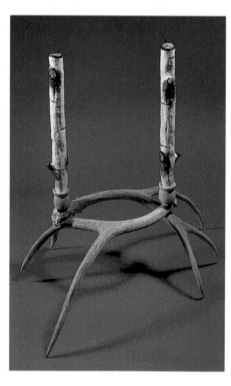

RIGHT

ANTLERS ARE ARRANGED TO FORM THE SPINY BASE OF THIS LAMP, WHICH AT ONE TIME MAY HAVE BELONGED IN AN OLD LODGE OR RESORT. THE UNUSUAL SHADE WAS MADE FROM A BEACON BLANKET AND TRIMMED WITH PINK SILK FRINGE. THE LAMP IS NOW IN THE MONGERSON-WUNDERLICH COLLECTION.

WESTERN-STYLE ARCHITECTURE

THE SHAPE OF THE WEST

Those who migrated from the East must have experienced a kind of culture shock when they confronted the frontier's vastness. They left behind dense forests, which easily provided wood for shelter, only to find the sameness of sod. Yet, with the true grit of that early westering spirit came a native architecture. Writers H. Keith Sawyers and David Murphy, in their 1986 essay on Nebraska's architectural frontier, call it "making somewhere out of nowhere."

The expansiveness of the vistas at first dwarfed any style of architecture. The mission was simply to create a fortification against the elements. Gradually, the West became a grand mixture of ethnic building traditions. Just as you could tell a cowboy's region by his chaps and hat, so too could you define a region by its architecture. Each style was a

ABOVE: A LOG CABIN IN NEW MEXICO.
OPPOSITE: A WYOMING DWELLING BY ALPINE LOG HOMES.

response to the environment: adobe for the sun-drenched Southwest, log cabins for the Rockies, and gingerbread Victorian houses for Colorado, parts of Texas, and the California coast.

Each group that settled a region—the German-Russians in Texas and the Dakotas, the Poles and Moravians in Nebraska, the Mormons in Utah, the Native Americans and Hispanics in New Mexico, Colorado, and California—brought its own architectural traditions. The common denominator was the materials at hand and the quest to create a community. Whether building with mud or wood, the pioneers adapted to a hostile, unyielding environment.

Where wood was scarce, sod and clay became the staple of frontier architecture. Mixed with loam, straw, water, grass, sand, or wool, it was shaped into a brick and dried in the sun.

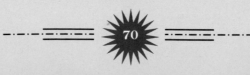

ABOVE: SOD WAS OFTEN MIXED WITH MATERIALS TO ADD A MEASURE OF DURABILITY, AS IN THIS PIONEER HOME IN LINCOLN, NEW MEXICO.

Puddled-clay walls, shaped by hand with fieldstone, twigs, and sticks as filler, were another innovation. So was rammed earth—puddled clay packed between forms. The latter enjoyed a revival in the 1970s as earth-sheltered homes responded to ecological and environmental concerns. These homes bear little resemblance to their primitive ancestors. Still, despite different designs and intent, their origins are the same.

Many of those early sod houses have, in "dust to dust" fashion, returned to the place of their genesis. Some survive as relics of the West's early architectural history; others are preserved in family photo albums.

The Spanish introduced adobe brick at the beginning of the 17th century. It is a sturdy survivor of this early architectural form. Adobe materials were cheaper than rock or stone, readily available, and quick to make as long as the sun was shining. Small dwellings could be constructed in a few days; a dozen might be built to house migrant workers.

Lime plaster was often the finishing coating for adobe bricks. The resulting structures were easy to maintain and fairly resistant to fire.

As much as the West loves its adobes, it is also enamored of cabins in the woods, rustic hunting lodges, and grand homes built of logs lining mountainsides and sheltered in lush valleys. The inevitable marriage of adobe and logs occurred when Fort Marcy Stockade was built in Santa Fe in 1846. Stucco dressed the log interior.

The railroads made possible a wider choice of building materials and greater diversity of architectural styles. They brought fired brick and glass, milled dimensional lumber, and sawed boards, allowing more creativity in roofs, structural supports, windows, and doors. Also, they fostered false-front architecture, as transplanted Easterners created

ABOVE: THIS TRADITIONAL STUCCO HOME IN "DECO RIVAL" STYLE REFLECTS A 1930S TREND. *OPPOSITE:* OLD-FASHIONED RUSTIC COMFORT AND LOG-CABIN INGENUITY ARE EVIDENT AT THE KOOTENAI LODGE IN SWAN LAKE, MONTANA. LOGS MAKE A DRAMATIC STATEMENT, WHETHER THEY ARE USED FOR SUPPORT BEAMS, LOFT RAILINGS, OR BASIC CONSTRUCTION.

ABOVE: IN THE EARLY DAYS OF THE WEST, THE MOST HUMBLE DWELLINGS BECAME HOME—
HOWEVER MAKESHIFT OR TRANSIENT. THIS PHOTO FROM THE KINGSTON COLLECTION DEPICTS A
CROW INDIAN ENCAMPMENT, CIRCA 1890.

instant cities on the prairies. In railroad towns and mining camps, as the West's architecture began to come of age, the word *façade* acquired a whole new meaning.

Many false-front towns were short-lived, subject to the vagaries of fortune that made the towns flourish in the first place. Those false-front towns represented an intimate architectural style and were a symbol, for a short time, of urbanization.

As lumber became plentiful, dugouts and adobe gave way to gable-ended log structures, with mud chinking between the logs. Dirt floors, river-stone fireplaces, and cantilevered and shed roofs were common.

Spanish Colonial and California Mission styles reflect the Hispanic influence on the West. Built of frame, stucco, or stone, these pristine white homes have red or blue tiled roofs and graceful arches.

ABOVE: THE STANLEY HOTEL IS ONE OF THE WEST'S MOST FAMOUS LANDMARKS, BLENDING VICTORIAN AND FRENCH ARCHITECTURAL THEMES. IT IS LOCATED IN ESTES PARK, COLORADO.

Monterey style, blending Anglo, Spanish, and Greek Revival motifs, is two stories with a cantilevered second-floor porch. Many such homes appear to have been built in a sprawling pattern; usually they grew in stages, according to the owner's wealth and needs. In New Mexico, Arizona, and West Texas, Territorial

ABOVE: THE EXTERIOR OF THE HISTORIC GEORGE RESIDENCE IN PLANO, TEXAS, LITERALLY EXUDES VICTORIAN CHARM AND ELEGANCE WITH ITS GINGERBREAD AND MOLDINGS.

style was single story, with flat roofs and brick-crowned roof parapets.

Ranch style, which grew out of the tradition of 1930s dude ranches, blends with the landscape's vastness. A ranch house was usually a sprawling one-story horizontal or L-shaped structure, surrounded by a large spread of land. Ranch houses tended to be built of adobe, log, or stone or sometimes a combination of all three. The true Ranch-style house always had a fireplace, as the hearth was the hub of

ABOVE: THE SANTA BARBARA CITY HALL IS A CLASSIC EXAMPLE OF CULTURAL BLENDING. THE RED-TILE ROOF MIXES MEXICAN, SPANISH, AND MOORISH THEMES. THE COLUMNS REFLECT THE MORE-FORMAL CORINTHIAN STYLE, WHILE METALWORK RAILINGS EXPRESS A MODERN SENSIBILITY.

the home. Surrounding the house were outbuildings—a bunkhouse for cowboys, a corral, a barn, and sometimes a stable.

In the 1950s and '60s, Ranch-style houses became popular with builders, who tried to recreate the look of the West in smaller-scale tract housing. In today's "New West," architects create hybrids of traditional elements and contemporary innovation, greatly expanding the design horizon.

FROM CLIFF DWELLINGS TO LOG CABINS

liff dwellings and pueblos of New Mexico, Colorado, and Arizona hark back to the Anasazi Indian era of 2,000 years ago when architecture emerged like a fledgling child from the earth.

While pueblo communities still exist, the log cabin is the enduring example of the West's early architecture. Built from existing lumber to shelter inhabitants from the elements, log cabins were primitive, one-room buildings. Their contemporary counterparts may be either rustic or elaborate. Good examples are found in Fredericksburg,

Texas, a German-American community that made *fachwerk,* or decorative wood-on-wood inlays, a standard part of every log house.

Whether a rustic cabin is restored, built from a kit, or reinvented from the ground up, log homes now feature ceilings of pegged beams, speckled timber, trim made from hand-split poles, massive rock fireplaces, and cross beams wrapped with rawhide. Always, new log homes are designed as havens of rustic comfort to blend with the environment, whether perched on a mountain precipice or cloistered in a valley.

ABOVE: TOURISTS WHO VISIT THE CANYON OF GREAT HOUSES IN CHACO CULTURE NATIONAL HISTORIC PARK NEAR FARMINGTON, NEW MEXICO, CAN VIEW THE ADOBE-BRICK CONSTRUCTION OF PUEBLO BONITO, WHICH THRIVED IN 1100 A.D. IT WAS THE LARGEST VILLAGE IN CHACO CANYON, CONTAINING MORE THAN 600 ROOMS. HAND-HEWN LOGS SERVE AS *VIGAS* AND SUPPORT THE LABYRINTH OF DOORWAYS WINDING THROUGH THE PUEBLO, WHICH HOUSED AS MANY AS 1,200 PEOPLE. *OPPOSITE:* THE ANCIENT DWELLINGS IN MESA VERDE NATIONAL PARK ARE AN ARCHITECTURAL TREASURE, REVEALING THE INGENUITY OF THE ANASAZI INDIANS IN CREATING A CITY OF STONE IN A CLIFFSIDE ALCOVE. THE ANASAZI, WHOSE NAME MEANS "SOMEONE'S ANCESTORS" IN THE NAVAJO LANGUAGE, WERE PREHISTORIC SOUTHWESTERN PEOPLE WHO LIVED IN THE AREA WHERE UTAH, COLORADO, NEW MEXICO, AND ARIZONA MEET.

ABOVE LEFT

LADDERS WERE AND STILL ARE AN ESSENTIAL FUNCTIONAL TOOL IN PUEBLO LIFE.
THIS ONE, FASHIONED OF PEELED LOG, RESTS ATOP THE MESA AT NEW MEXICO'S ACOMA PUEBLO.
TODAY, LADDERS COME INSIDE AS AN ORNAMENTAL ACCESSORY, OFTEN SHOWCASING
BLANKETS AND OTHER COLLECTIBLE ITEMS.

ABOVE RIGHT

THE EVER-PRESENT LADDER LEADS INTO A KIVA IN A PUEBLO AT THE PECOS NATIONAL HISTORIC
MONUMENT. THE KIVA IS A CEREMONIAL CHAMBER WHERE TRADITIONAL SACRED CEREMONIES AND
RITUALS ARE CONDUCTED, USUALLY INVOLVING ONLY THE MALES OF THE TRIBE. THE LADDER IS
SHOWN LEANING AGAINST AN ALTAR OF ROCK.

ABOVE

THE INN AT LORETTO IN SANTA FE, NEW MEXICO, IS CONSTRUCTED LIKE AN OLD ADOBE PUEBLO, RISING IN STAIRSTEP FASHION OUT OF THE EARTH. THE DESIGN WAS INSPIRED BY THE TAOS PUEBLO, WHICH IS MORE THAN 900 YEARS OLD. IT IS A MAJOR TOURIST ATTRACTION IN THE SOUTHWEST.

LEFT

THE INFLUENCE OF GEOMETRIC SHAPES IS EVIDENT IN THIS SETTING, WHICH SHOWS A HORNO, OR OVEN MADE FROM ADOBE MIXED WITH STRAW, AND STAIRS RUNNING ALONGSIDE IT. AN ACOMA POT, IN TRADITIONAL BLACK, WHITE, AND ORANGE-RED COLORS, IS A FAVORITE ACCESSORY IN WESTERN-STYLE DECOR.

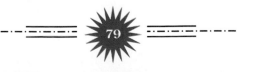

ABOVE

TOP LEFT: RUSTIC IS THE IMAGE SUGGESTED BY THIS WINDOW-AND-DOOR VIGNETTE FROM
AN EARLY RURAL LOG CABIN. *BOTTOM LEFT:* THIS HISTORIC LOG CABIN WAS BUILT AT THE BASE
OF A MOUNTAIN IN THE SAN ISABEL NATIONAL FOREST, WEST OF BUENA VISTA, COLORADO.
THE DWELLING FEATURES TRADITIONAL NOTCHED-LOG CONSTRUCTION. *RIGHT:* THIS LOG CABIN
PROVIDES A WARM RETREAT FROM A WINTER SNOW IN WEST BOULDER VALLEY, SOUTHEAST
OF LIVINGSTON, MONTANA.

OPPOSITE

BUILT TO ACCOMMODATE A LARGE FAMILY, THIS LOG HOME FEATURES A DECK FOR VIEWING
THE BEAUTIFUL SURROUNDING SCENERY. PINE TREES SERVE AS A CONTRASTING BACKDROP FOR
THE LOGS' TEXTURE. ABUNDANT WILDFLOWERS COMPLEMENT THE LOGS WITH THE EVER-CHANGING
COLORS OF NATURE.

FARMS AND RANCHES

Early-day farmhouses all across the West had but one architectural mission—shelter and survival on the frontier. Farmhouses reflected the stark simplicity of the farming lifestyle. Perhaps nowhere is there more uniformity of architecture than in the early farmhouses.

Although each region expressed the building traditions of the ethnic groups that settled it—Germans and Alsatians in Texas, Danes in California—there is a decided Franco-Germanic charm to these structures. Fashioned of native timber, clapboard, or stone, these houses had certain typical characteristics, such as limestone walls and a veranda or porch.

Today, architects erect new versions of these frontier outposts. But these modern-day "farmhouses" are more likely to have a guest house, a studio, and even a horse barn.

ABOVE: A DESERTED FARMHOUSE, GRACED BY COTTONWOOD AND CEDAR TREES, STANDS IN AN IDAHO HAY FIELD. *OPPOSITE:* THIS CONTEMPORARY HOME NEAR ALBUQUERQUE, DESIGNED BY ARCHITECT GARRETT SMITH AS HIS PERSONAL RESIDENCE, IS FASHIONED OF CORRUGATED SILVER TIN, REMINISCENT OF THE TIN ROOFS ON EARLY RANCHES AND FARMHOUSES. BROWN AND WHITE SPLIT-FACE BLOCKS ADD A COLORFUL CONTRAST.

The Ranch architectural style was inspired by dude ranches that drew Easterners westward. By the 1920s, dude-ranch vacations reached mythic proportions and fostered Ranch-style architecture.

Early ranch houses had hip roofs with tin sheeting and were surrounded by barns, stables, bunkhouses, chicken coops, storage sheds, and a corral. The low-slung, one-story style that flourished in 1950s tract houses was simpler, built for those who merely wished to imitate the Western lifestyle.

Leather, cowhide, and Navajo rugs and blankets find their place in today's ranches. The more successful the ranch, the more elaborate the furnishings, with Victorian or English imports attesting to the rancher's wealth. Just as important, though, we expect ranch houses to have a rambling, rugged simplicity and a warmly welcoming ambience.

OPPOSITE

A BLEND OF ANGLES CHARACTERIZES THIS HOME, WHICH IS SET AGAINST A FOREST OF PINE TREES. THE VERTICAL ASPECT OF THE L-SHAPED DESIGN IS SOFTENED BY THE HALF-MOON CURVE OF THE BLUE TIN ROOF ON THE FRONT WING. MANY FARMS AND RANCHES STILL HAVE METAL BUILDINGS WITH A HALF-MOON-CURVED ROOF.

ABOVE

THIS EXTERIOR VIEW OF THIS RESIDENCE IN BIG FORK, MONTANA, DESIGNED BY JERRY LOCATI, SHOWS HOW THE VARIOUS TEXTURAL ELEMENTS WORK TOGETHER FOR A TRUE WESTERN LODGE OR RANCH LOOK. THE STACKED-STONE PILLARS AND RED-CEDAR SUPPORT BEAMS ARE INTEGRAL DESIGN ELEMENTS, AS ARE THE SIMPLE LOW SHRUBS.

RIGHT

ARCHITECT NEIL WRIGHT TOOK ADVANTAGE OF A MOUNTAIN SETTING FOR THIS SUN VALLEY, IDAHO, HOME. THIS PHOTO, TAKEN AT SUNSET, SHOWS THE VASTNESS OF THE RANCH-STYLE HOUSE AND ITS NUMEROUS INDOOR AND OUTDOOR ENTERTAINING AREAS.

Victorian's Romantic Gingerbread

Victorian architecture seems a curiosity amid the rough-and-tumble terrain of the West. But from Aspen, Colorado, to Eureka, California, it is an ornate gingerbread reminder of how settlers imported design traditions of the East, no doubt in order to feel more at home.

With all its flamboyance, Victorian architecture gave a much-needed sense of formality and tradition as frontier towns were shaping their architectural character. Especially in California, Victorian-style homes were a symbol of prosperity, of fortunes made in the gold and silver fields.

Victorian is a patchwork, blending Gothic Revival, French Second Empire, Queen Anne, and Italianate in tiered designs that remind one of wedding cakes. Hallmarks include the mixed use of columns, capitals, and *corbels,* vivid trim colors, decorative shingles, gabled and hipped roofs, balconies, friezes, leaded window panes, and stained glass. Decorative window hoods are almost always complemented by intricately patterned lace curtains peeking from windows.

In contemporary translations, the Victorian style still evokes the splendor and elegance of the late 19th century. Modern Victorian dwellings also reflect a revived interest in architectural preservation, especially in California and Colorado.

Above: The architectural symmetry of San Francisco's Victorian homes shows the rhythm and charm of this style. *Opposite:* The contrast of new and old is seen in these Victorian residences on San Francisco's Steiner Street.

TOP LEFT

THE MOLLY BROWN HOUSE IN DENVER, COLORADO, BLENDS STONE AND WOOD TO PROVIDE A CLASSIC EXAMPLE OF AN EARLY VICTORIAN HOME. A FRIEZE OF ROMAN CHARIOTEERS, CHISELED IN ROCK, SHOWS THE WIDE-RANGING CULTURAL INFLUENCES ON WESTERN ARCHITECTURE.

BOTTOM LEFT

A VIGNETTE OF THE GEORGE RESIDENCE SHOWS THE DETAIL THAT BUILDERS LAVISHED ON THE VICTORIAN STYLE. THE HOME WAS BUILT IN 1900 AND FEATURES THE TRADITIONAL EMBELLISHMENTS OF GINGERBREAD TRIM AND SCROLLWORK.

BOTTOM RIGHT

LAYERS OF ARCHITECTURAL DETAIL, DELINEATED BY VIVID COLORS, HAVE GIVEN VICTORIAN ARCHITECTURE THE NICKNAME "PAINTED LADY." IN THE ELEGANT STRUCTURES SHOWN HERE IN LOS ANGELES'S HERITAGE SQUARE, THE ORNATE TRIM IS ENHANCED BY A BRIGHT MIX OF JADE AND BLUE, TERRA COTTA AND SALMON. EVEN THE STORAGE SHED IN THE FOREGROUND SPORTS DECORATIVE ELEMENTS.

OPPOSITE

LESS ELABORATE BUT STILL REFLECTING THE VICTORIAN THEME, THIS SOUTHWESTERN HOME SHOWS OTHER INFLUENCES, RANGING FROM A MODIFIED FRENCH MANSARD ROOF TO THE RED BRICK COMMON AMONG HOMES FROM GERMAN FARM COMMUNITIES IN TEXAS. A TRACE OF THE FRONTIER QUEEN ANNE STYLE IS ALSO EVIDENT.

FRENCH, RUSSIAN, ART DECO, AND ART NOUVEAU

The great fusion of architectural influences on the West extended well beyond East Coast themes to include the inspiration of Europe and international art movements. While less prominent than Victorian, French and Russian influences played a supporting role in this drama.

Architectural symmetry is the mistress of French construction. From that Old World heritage comes a harmonious blending of stacked stone, brick and wood, central entryways, arched French doors, detailed dormers, and heavily shingled wood roofs—often mansard style—with copper finials.

Onion domes are the architectural symbols of Moscow and St. Petersburg, and a few made their way to the West, particularly in colder climates. Most Russian buildings are made of stone and concrete with a stucco finish, painted several shades of ocher with stone arches in white or a light shade. The most common Russian import, however, is jigsaw detailing that originated in Siberia. Turn-of-the-century ghost towns throughout Colorado have this element, seen in weathered wood, *corbels,* and square lines.

ABOVE: FRENCH AND GOTHIC INFLUENCES ABOUND IN SANTA FE'S 19TH-CENTURY LORETTO CHAPEL, NOTED FOR ITS UNIQUE SPIRAL STAIRCASE BUILT WITHOUT SUPPORTS.

A classic example of the blend of Russian and Southwest themes is best seen at the Fechin Institute in Taos, New Mexico. The home was built in the late 1920s by the Russian-born artist Nicolai Fechin and blends the flesh-colored adobe exterior indigenous to Taos with interior wood carvings that reveal Fechin's Russian heritage. The home is now maintained by his daughter, Eya Branham.

The severe geometric look of Art Deco, born of a 1925 exhibition of decorative arts in Paris, and Art Nouveau, with its leaflike forms and sinuous lines, are two other European influences. Art Deco and Art Nouveau lamps have often been coupled with rustic furnishings. But it is the architecture of this period—pristine white or stucco exteriors emblazoned with ornamentation, friezes, and decorative tiles—that rivals the Victorian style for originality. Examples can be found from Albuquerque, New Mexico, to Tulsa, Oklahoma, to Miami Beach, Florida.

ABOVE: THE FECHIN HOUSE IS A TRIBUTE TO THE ARTIST'S EXUBERANT LOVE OF ALL FORMS OF ART.
FROM HIS PAINTINGS WITH THEIR VIVID COLORS TO THE INTRICATE DETAILS OF HIS WOOD CARVING
AND SCULPTURES, THE HOUSE AND ITS MYRIAD COLLECTIONS EXPRESS FECHIN'S ARTISTIC VITALITY.
HIS WORK HAS INSPIRED NUMEROUS ARTISTS, INCLUDING JEREMY MORELLI, WHO NOW DOES
ADAPTATIONS OF FECHIN'S CARVED DOORS. MORELLI'S WORK IS TO BE FEATURED
IN THE NEW FECHIN INN, CURRENTLY UNDER CONSTRUCTION IN TAOS.

ABOVE

THE LENSIC THEATRE IN SANTA FE,
NEW MEXICO, EXPRESSES AN ELABORATE
ARCHITECTURAL STYLE. RICH SPANISH
COLONIAL INFLUENCES ARE SEEN IN
MOORISH-STYLE WINDOWS, THE SHELL
MOTIF, AND THE DETAILING THAT
SURROUNDS THE ROOF.

LEFT

"ORNAMENT" IS AN APPROPRIATE NAME
FOR THIS SHOP HOUSED IN THE LENSIC, WITH
ITS STRONG SPANISH COLONIAL INFLUENCE.
THE WHITE STUCCO WALLS ARE A STAGE FOR
THE BLACK WROUGHT-IRON GRILLWORK,
ARCHED WINDOWS, AND DECORATIVE
MOLDING OVER THE FRONT DOOR.

ABOVE

THE KI MO THEATRE WAS DESIGNED BY INEZ WESTLAKE, WHO DREW HER INSPIRATION FOR THE SHIELD MOTIF FROM HOPI ARTIST NAMPEYO. ELABORATELY PAINTED SPINDLES SET OFF THE SHIELDS THAT OUTLINE THE THIRD-STORY WINDOWS.

LEFT

THE EXTERIOR OF THE KI MO THEATRE IN ALBUQUERQUE, NEW MEXICO, MELDS ADOBE AND ART DECO INFLUENCES. ARCHITECTS ROBERT AND CARL BOLLER BUILT THE THEATER IN 1927 OF REINFORCED BRICK, HEAVILY STUCCOED TO RESEMBLE ADOBE PLASTER.

CALIFORNIA MISSION ARCHITECTURE

Chapels and mission churches that appeared in coastal California towns as early as the mid-18th century were built in a style inspired by the Hispanic culture that followed the Catholic padres north along the *Camino Real* during the 1700s.

The English poet and artist William Morris once wrote that all architecture had a duty to reform society through honest craftsmanship, truthful use of materials, and forthright application of structural systems. As the West was settled, people desired an architecture suggestive of a settled look, a sense of order, and at least the illusion of prosperity.

That settled look, with its blend of cultural influences, is best seen in the California Mission style, whether expressed in rambling church missions or sprawling *haciendas*.

The Mission style is characterized by thick, curved walls, white or buff exteriors, interior dark woods, tile roofs, central courtyards, domes, and bell towers. Current adaptations may be smaller but no less graceful, as Mission architecture today enjoys a romantic revival, not only throughout the West, but all over the country.

ABOVE: RANCHO SAN CARLOS, NEAR CARMEL VALLEY, CALIFORNIA, IS ONE OF THE FEW OLD CALIFORNIA RANCHES STILL INTACT AT A TIME WHEN MANY OF THE WEST'S GREAT SPREADS HAVE BEEN BROKEN UP. THE 20,000-ACRE RANCH WITH ITS 37-ROOM *HACIENDA* IS ONE OF THE LARGEST PRIVATE LAND HOLDINGS AND PRESERVES ON THE CENTRAL CALIFORNIA COAST.

Above: THE WEST'S MOST PROMINENT EXAMPLE OF SPANISH COLONIAL ARCHITECTURE IS THE SAN XAVIER DEL BAC MISSION IN TUCSON, ARIZONA. THE CHURCH IS AN UNUSUAL BLEND OF BYZANTINE, MOORISH, AND MEXICAN BAROQUE STYLES AND CLASSICAL MOTIFS. DETAILED ORNAMENTAL CARVINGS, EMBELLISHED WITH POLYCHROME PAINTING, GRACE THE IMPRESSIVE AND ORNATE FAÇADE.

Below: THE STARK LINES OF ADOBE ARCHITECTURE ARE COMPLEMENTED BY THE ARCHES, BALUSTRADES, AND DECORATIVE DETAILING OF THE SAN XAVIER DEL BAC MISSION. NOT SURPRISINGLY, IT IS OFTEN CALLED "THE WHITE DOVE OF THE DESERT."

LEFT

TOP: SMALL ARCHWAYS, MUCH LIKE DORMER WINDOWS, ARE CARVED INTO THE THICK ADOBE WALLS TO SHELTER THE ARCHED WINDOWS IN THE CLOCK TOWER OF THE SANTA BARBARA, CALIFORNIA, COUNTY COURTHOUSE. *BOTTOM:* THE MISSION AT SANTA BARBARA, CALIFORNIA, FEATURES A PORTAL LINED WITH STONE PILLARS, *VIGAS* THAT FORM THE CEILING, AND BRICKS THAT PAVE THE WALKWAY.

RIGHT

TOP: THE SANTA BARBARA COURTHOUSE IS AN ORNATE EXAMPLE OF THE CALIFORNIA MISSION STYLE. *BOTTOM:* SPANISH COLONIAL AND CALIFORNIA MISSION THEMES BLEND WITH MOORISH AND RUSSIAN MOTIFS IN THE OLD GUARD HOUSE OF SANTA BARBARA'S HISTORIC EL PRESIDIO.

OPPOSITE

THE PATIOS, WALKWAYS, AND WELL-MANICURED GROUNDS OF VILLA PHILMONT AND THE PHILMONT MUSEUM INVITE VISITORS TO STROLL THE GROUNDS AND ENJOY THE SURROUNDING SCENERY. *INSET:* VILLA PHILMONT WAS BUILT OF SOLID MASONRY WITH A ROOF OF MULTICOLORED TILES AND BLUE WROUGHT-IRON GATES ACCENTING THE PATIO WITH ITS FLAGSTONE WALKWAYS. THE HOME WAS COMPLETED IN 1927.

ABOVE

THE SUBTLE INFLUENCE OF PUEBLO-STYLE ARCHITECTURE IS SEEN IN THIS CONTEMPORARY
ADAPTATION OF THE CALIFORNIA MISSION STYLE. WHITE-STUCCO WALLS AND A RED-TILE ROOF
HONOR A LONGSTANDING ARCHITECTURAL TRADITION. THE RECTANGULAR WINDOWS AND
RECTANGULAR POOL OUTLINED BY A STAIRSTEP WALL ADD A DISTINCTLY MODERN TOUCH.

OPPOSITE

THE CALIFORNIA MISSION AND SPANISH COLONIAL STYLES COMBINE TO SUGGEST A
TRADITIONAL TOWNHOUSE THEME IN THIS CALIFORNIA HOME. THE CURVING SHAPES OF THE RED
ROOF TILES ADD VISUAL AND TEXTURAL INTEREST TO THE STRAIGHT LINES OF THE HOME.

THE ENDURING ADOBES

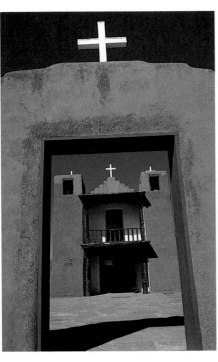

ABOVE: THE HUMBLE TEXTURE AND SIMPLE
SHAPES OF ADOBE MISSION STYLE ARE
EVIDENT IN TAOS, NEW MEXICO'S
ST. GERONIMO CHURCH. STARK WHITE
CROSSES ARE SILHOUETTED AGAINST THE SKY.
HAND-CARVED ORNAMENTATION IS SEEN IN
THE PORCH SUPPORTS AND RAILINGS. THE
STAIR-STEP MOTIF LEADS TO THE MISSION'S
CENTRAL CROSS.

I f only the ancient adobe dwellings could talk. What insights and memories they could share with us about the early architectural history of the Southwest. These structures, like Santa Fe's oldest house or the Rios-Caledonia Adobe in San Miguel, California, evoke a sense of the past.

Most had thatched roofs, packed-dirt floors, and two- to three-foot-thick walls laid on foundations of loose stone. Their presence in today's world is a construction phenomenon peculiar to the Southwest.

These structures of earth and water—more than 50,000 in the Southwest—have a timeless charm, whether the adobe has lineage or is newly poured.

No longer primitive in appearance, new adobe homes have such elaborate amenities as tile roofs, wood flooring, chimneys, balconies, and tinted plaster for outside walls. *Vigas, latillas,* and *corbels* are standard features. Glass windows provide expansive views of the majestic scenery. Graceful doorways always whisper warm welcomes.

ABOVE: THE ARCHITECTURAL DRAMA OF
ADOBE CONSTRUCTION IS SEEN IN THE
ENTRANCE TO THIS ECLECTIC NEW WEST-
STYLE HOME. *OPPOSITE:* WOOD, GLASS,
ADOBE, AND CEDAR BLEND BEAUTIFULLY IN
THIS ALBUQUERQUE, NEW MEXICO,
RESIDENCE, DESIGNED BY GARRETT SMITH,
LTD. OPEN WOOD BEAMS PROVIDE A FAUX
CEILING AT THE ENTRANCE.

ABOVE

THIS SANTA FE HOME FEATURES LOW, ONE-STORY CONSTRUCTION, WITH DARK-BROWN WOODEN BEAMS AND SHUTTERS ACCENTING THE TAWNY COLOR OF THE ADOBE.

RIGHT

STUCCO WALLS, RED-TILE ROOFS, AND WROUGHT-IRON RAILINGS ARE HALLMARKS OF WESTERN-STYLE ARCHITECTURE, BLENDING SPANISH, MOORISH, AND MEXICAN INFLUENCES.

OPPOSITE

ARCHITECT JACKIE MOWRY EXPRESSED A TRADITIONAL ARCHITECTURAL THEME IN THIS HISTORIC ADOBE HOME IN SANTA FE, NEW MEXICO.

ABOVE

A SOFT PINK HUE IN THE NATIVE STONE CONTRASTS BEAUTIFULLY WITH
THE BLUE SKY AND RUGGED LANDSCAPE. THE STREAMLINED
ARCHITECTURAL STYLE SUGGESTS SUBTLE INSPIRATION FROM ARCHITECT
FRANK LLOYD WRIGHT'S DESIGNS.

LEFT

CHAIRS SUCH AS THESE WITH WOVEN LEATHER STRIPS FOR A BASE ARE
COMMONLY FOUND IN SOUTHWEST HOMES AND RESTAURANTS. THE STEEL
SUPPORT BEAM FEATURES A LIGHT WELL AT THE TOP THAT ILLUMINATES
THE UNDERSIDE OF THE BALCONY. THE ROOF HAS STEEL TRIM. THE PATIO
RAILING IS OF WOOD.

OPPOSITE

THIS SANTA FE TOWNHOUSE DESIGNED BY ARCHITECT DORMAN/BREEN
OF SANTA FE AND ALBUQUERQUE IS BASED ON TRADITIONAL PUEBLO-
STYLE ARCHITECTURE. A GARDEN OF WILDFLOWERS AND HOLLYHOCKS
PROVIDES A CONTRAST TO THE RICH SAND COLOR OF THE WALLS.

LEFT

Corbels add architectural interest to buildings of the Southwest, as seen in the Federal Building in Santa Fe, New Mexico (*top*) and in La Casita (*second from top*), by architect John Douglas. Colorful doors and windows contrast the subdued shades of adobe in this Santa Fe dwelling (*third from top*), while a luxuriant garden (*bottom*) relieves the simple adobe façade of this Arizona residence designed by Adolf deRoy Mark.

RIGHT

Top: Old-fashioned shutters with metal hinges add a touch of architectural history to La Casita. The stark simplicity of the structure is highlighted by the spiny beauty of the tall cactus. *Bottom:* This view of Adolf deRoy Mark's design shows the entrance across a foot bridge fording an active desert wash, filled with seasonal flora. A traditional Moorish entrance pavilion greets—and refreshes—the tired desert traveler. A guest house is attached to the main house by a loggia and wall, but is completely self-contained for privacy. All bedrooms have an intimate adjoining garden.

OPPOSITE

Pine trees indigenous to New Mexico frame this contemporary residence. Curved walls lend an aura of mystery to the home, hiding patios and interior walkways and providing a sense of seclusion for the owners.

THE ECLECTICISM OF THE NEW WEST

ontemporary architects are in the business of building dreams that people live in. And with more than a third of all Americans considering themselves Western enthusiasts, architects are giving form to what is fancied the national character.

In fact, today's architects are basing designs on historical dwellings at the same time that they are introducing innovative details and materials. Chrome, plastics, glass, ceramic tile, mirrors, and neon add dramatic postmodern themes that would have been

pooh-poohed by Westerners only a few decades ago.

Among the standard bearers of this new look are homes with an environmentally sensitive design incorporating landscape restoration and materials that mirror the natural beauty of a site. The style can be either starkly modern or primitive adobe echoing the rhythm of surrounding mountains. Other features include decks, indoor and outdoor fireplaces, spacious gallerylike rooms, and an abundant use of pine—all contributing to the sense of light-filled spaciousness that is the West's essence.

ABOVE: THE TRADITIONAL MEANDERING STACKED LOOK OF PUEBLO-STYLE ARCHITECTURE HAS BEEN REINTERPRETED BY ARCHITECT JON ANDERSON IN DRAMATIC CONTEMPORARY LINES IN THIS WESTERN-STYLE HOME IN ALBUQUERQUE. *OPPOSITE:* FLOOR-TO-CEILING WINDOW SQUARES CREATE A DRAMATIC ARCHITECTURAL THEME IN THIS HOME IN THE TINNIN FARMS AREA OF ALBUQUERQUE, DESIGNED BY JON ANDERSON. THE RESIDENCE, NEAR THE RIO GRANDE RIVER, IS GRACED BY TALL RIVERINE COTTONWOODS.

ABOVE

THIS VIEW OF ARCHITECT HOLMES SABATINI'S DESIGN, LOCATED IN THE TANOAN AREA OF ALBUQUERQUE, SHOWS THE HARMONIOUS BLEND OF ARCHITECTURAL THEMES AND DESIGN MATERIALS. STEEL, STUCCO, MARBLE, AND TILE ALL COMBINE WITH THE REFLECTIVE BEAUTY OF GLASS FOR POSTMODERN DESIGN ELEGANCE.

OPPOSITE

WOOD, STUCCO, AND STEEL ACCENT THE VAST EXPANSE AT THE HOME'S ENTRANCE. ARCHITECT SABATINI, WITH OFFICES IN ALBUQUERQUE, NEW MEXICO, AND LAS VEGAS, NEVADA, USED FREE-FLOWING GEOMETRIC FORMS FOR HIS POSTMODERN DESIGN. THE HOME, WHICH SITS ON A HILL OVERLOOKING A GOLF COURSE, PROVIDES A VIEW OF THE SANDIA MOUNTAINS.

ABOVE

HIGH-TECH, FUTURISTIC ARCHITECTURE IS SET AGAINST THE RUGGED MOUNTAINS OF ALBUQUERQUE FOR THIS RESIDENCE DESIGNED BY ARCHITECT DORMAN/BREEN. WHITE-STUCCO WALLS ARE ACCENTED BY VAST EXPANSES OF GLASS, WITH ROUND DECKS AND MODERNISTIC RAILINGS BLENDING THE BEAUTIES OF NATURE WITH THE BEST OF CONTEMPORARY DESIGN.

RIGHT

LOOKING MUCH LIKE A FUTURISTIC SPACE STATION, THE SAME RESIDENCE EMPLOYS THE LATEST HIGH-TECH INNOVATIONS IN WESTERN DESIGN. THE SYNTHETIC-GRANITE EXTERIOR ECHOES THE MASSIVE FEEL OF BOULDERS.

OPPOSITE

THE ANCIENT NATURAL ARCHITECTURE OF RED ROCK CANYONS IN SEDONA, ARIZONA, MAKES AN INCREDIBLE BACKDROP FOR THE DESIGNS OF ALBUQUERQUE ARCHITECT BARRY LANGFORD. THIS HOME IS MADE OF SPLIT-FACED BLOCK AND STUCCO AND UTILIZES THE VOCABULARY OF THE NATURAL ENVIRONMENT. THE HOME IS SITUATED NEAR A NATURE AND WILDLIFE PRESERVE; DEER ARE FREQUENT GUESTS ON THE PROPERTY. LANDSCAPING IS INTENTIONALLY MINIMAL.

ABOVE LEFT

AN ART DECO YET POSTMODERN THEME IS EXPRESSED IN THIS HOME'S DESIGN. THE CURVING STAIRWAY AND ITS CONTEMPORARY WHITE-IRON RAILING SOFTEN THE STARK LINES OF THE EXTERIOR, AS DOES THE ARCH ACCENTING THE MAIN ENTRYWAY.

ABOVE RIGHT

THIS VIEW OF THE SAME HOME, SEEN FROM INSIDE THE CURVED FRONT ENTRANCE, SHOWS HOW THE DESIGN OF THE EXTERIOR RAILING HAS BEEN REINTERPRETED IN WOOD.

ABOVE

THIS SOUTHWEST RESIDENCE, WITH GUEST HOUSE, WAS DESIGNED TO RISE OUT OF THE
LANDSCAPE. THE LATE HARVEY HOSHAUR OF ALBUQUERQUE, NEW MEXICO, DESIGNED THE
MAIN STRUCTURE. BLENDING GEOMETRIC ANGLES, THE HOME IS FUELED BY SOLAR ENERGY, A
COMMON FEATURE OF WESTERN-STYLE DWELLINGS.

INTERIOR DESIGN

WESTERN SPOKEN HERE

Interior design with a Western flavor has evolved from its early sparse utilitarianism to today's eclectic celebration of all things Western. Whether the mood is one of fun-loving cowboy kitsch or the quiet beauty of museum-quality art and artifacts, Western design strives to bring a piece of the landscape, and a portion of our historical past, inside the home to become the next generation's family heirlooms.

At the root of Western interior design is a sense of authenticity. It is, after all, a look that seems indigenous to the West (though many might argue that Western design is merely a state of mind). For some of us, the fascination with Western design is rooted in memories of where we grew up. For others, it is a look inspired by Western novels and history books now yellowed with age, by movies and television series that have etched on our minds an indelible, if idealized, image of the West. Perhaps most important, the sense of Western design springs from priceless treasures and time-worn stories passed by raconteurs with relish—and exaggeration—from one generation to the next.

Whether we choose to dress our homes with artifacts, reproductions, or memorabilia gleaned from antique stores, flea markets, or family attics, each element of Western interior design represents in some way a piece of our collective national history, a relic of the most celebrated region of the country and the most honest of lifestyles. The evolution from everyday item (or even piece of junk) to *objet d'art* is usually quite simple—a Navajo rug or blanket, or a hand-pieced quilt, or a long-forgotten bleached cattle skull might be hung on a wall or propped on a shelf as a form of ornamentation. Suddenly, there is a new use—and new meaning—for a defunct item.

That transition from function to decoration is the prime characteristic of Western interior design. Remnants of the past and artifacts that were once purely useful—copper pots and baskets, stoneware and spurs—now take their place in this exciting design drama that pays tribute to the always colorful, sometimes poignant heritage of the West, while keeping a watchful eye on the future.

Like architecture, Western design is an amalgam that blends the intrigue and strength of the cowboy lifestyle with all the rustic earthiness of country

OPPOSITE: THE RESIDENCE OF SCULPTOR JOHN MORTENSEN IN WILSON, WYOMING, REVEALS HIS LOVE OF THE WEST.

ABOVE: A CHILD'S WOOL *SERAPE* FEATURES A NAVAJO DESIGN OF CROSSES, GEOMETRIC TRIANGLES, AND DIAMOND SHAPES. THE WEAVING BELONGS TO THE HEARD MUSEUM IN PHOENIX, ARIZONA.

living. It honors the tradition-filled legacies left by ancient Indian civilizations, and it invites the treasures from cultures as diverse as oriental and English to coexist harmoniously. Western design then becomes a melting pot of all the influences that shaped the West and created its myths and legends, its realities and peculiarities.

Western interior design draws its color palette from the mosaic of the landscape—the rich celadon of cactus and sage, the lush green of summer meadows, the intense gold of maize and sunflowers and crookneck squash, the vibrant blue of cornflowers and lupines, the brilliant reds of Navajo weavings, the translucent fuchsia of bougainvillea.

And always, each paintbrush image is set against the backdrop of bleached sand and stone, the red and brown strata of earth, the dark greens of spruce and pine-covered hillsides, the awesome gray of craggy mountain peaks, and the luminous shades of an ever-changing sky—that happy hunting ground of Indian legends.

Equally important are the many shades of wood, which is a focal point in almost every Western interior design. Nowhere does it play such a major role as in the log and white-washed pine beams and *corbels,* thick *vigas,* and skinny *latillas* that bring the earth inside to enhance the rustic charm of interior design. Weathered pine planking, old barn wood, and rough-sawed timber line the walls of many Western homes. Rock finds its place, too, usually in fireplaces.

From the front doors of the West, which so often bespeak the design personality to be found inside, to the decks overlooking broad, magnificent vistas, Western interior design borrows quaint themes from yesterday and places them in the contemporary spirit of today. Always there is the suggestion of

ABOVE: MISSION-STYLE INFLUENCES ARE SEEN IN THE ARCHITECTURE AND IN THE GRACEFULLY CURVED ARCHWAY OF THIS DOOR.
OPPOSITE: LOG BEAMS FORM A PATTERN OF VISUAL INTEREST IN THIS CONTEMPORARY WESTERN ENTRANCE.

ABOVE: NATIVE AMERICAN ARTIFACTS ARE PRESENTED, GALLERY STYLE, IN THIS HOME'S HALLWAY.

relaxed ease, comfort, and gracious yet informal hospitality.

Western design is also not without caprice. An old drugstore Indian moves indoors to a residential entryway from its previous home as a greeter for an Indian curio shop. Kachina dolls, once the ceremonial companions of Native American children, now dance across the top of a hearth or create a fanciful headboard. Caricatures of early-day cowboy scenes march around a lamp shade or decorate a chenille cowboy bedspread that would have made Hopalong

Cassidy right proud. Old deer hooves are refashioned as a vase. An ordinary tree limb becomes the trunk of a floor lamp.

Inevitably, a fascination with Western design moves us beyond the boundaries of our own environment, pushing us out of any sentimental time warp, nudging us beyond more than a passing fancy for this style. From that first look at an abandoned farmhouse or artifact to its eventual restoration, the process of falling in love with the trappings of the historical West forever changes how we live.

For some of us, the early fascination with Western design matures into a mission to preserve the many facets of Western culture. The quest evolves into a personal, heartfelt commitment to historical authenticity as we recreate, in our own homes and communities, a skillfully woven narrative of the past and the present.

And in so doing, we also design and create a new future for Western expression.

ABOVE: THE FUNCTIONAL ASPECT OF WESTERN DESIGN IS SEEN IN THIS THREE-DRAWER CHEST BY BERKELEY MILLS OF SANTA FE.
OPPOSITE: THIS WHITEFISH, MONTANA, HOME HAS A WRAPAROUND DECK AND ADIRONDACK-STYLE FURNITURE.

KITCHENS

THE HEART OF THE HOME

Western kitchens are much more than places to cook and bake. They are the rooms where family members and friends are also nourished by the convivial atmosphere. The kitchen may be resplendent with state-of-the-art conveniences and skylights, or it may be graced by an old cast-iron stove and speckleware cooking utensils. Still, the mood is one of cozy, comfortable charm. In the West, the kitchen—*la cocina*—is the hearth that draws families together.

Think of the kitchen as the "town square" of a home. It is here that gossip and advice and loving thoughts are issued with the same care that one serves tasty tortillas, enchiladas, Mexican wedding cookies, and hot chocolate. The character of a Western-style home is often defined by the spirit of its kitchen.

And it is in the kitchen that a potage of design ideas seems right at home. It is also the perfect place to show off. Open up the doors to the cupboards, arrange your collections—and display earthenware pitchers, a favorite aunt's majolica plates, treasured teapots from your grandmother. Old worktables, showing traces of their original buttermilk paint and scars that came from years of use, will be at home here. Pioneer artifacts and copper pots, hanging from a decorative rack or artfully arranged on the walls, are commonplace accessories. Antique cowboy dishes and railroad china peer from wooden plate racks, stout buffets, open shelving, or simple wooden cupboards. Wooden utensils stand ready in crockery pots. Pie safes with punched-tin designs, antique cupboards, Welsh dressers, and dry sinks hold kitchen treasures. Windowsills are filled with pots of fresh herbs or wildflowers. Mexican-tile backsplashes, plump *ristras* of red chiles, colorful corncobs, and gourds are Western kitchen signatures.

Chandeliers are as central to kitchen design as they are to living and dining rooms. Avoid the traditional, however. Antler, pottery, and candle motifs are some of the most popular. A sofa or comfortable overstuffed chairs nestle close to a fireplace, offering warmth and a place of conversation around the hearth, suggesting the homey ambience for which the West is known.

Cookbooks have a place of honor, savored as much for their literary appeal as their food and entertainment value. Who hasn't yearned for a day to curl up in a favorite kitchen chair, with a cup of hot coffee or tea at hand, and pass the time reading a cookbook as if it were a good mystery or romance?

Author M. Scott Momaday once called Taos, New Mexico, "the soul of the Southwest." Surely he wouldn't mind if we borrowed his phrase and said the kitchen is the soul, spirit, and spice of every home that is seasoned with Western design.

ABOVE: IF ONE BELIEVES THE FIREPLACE IS THE HEART OF THE HOME, THIS SETTING IS A TRUE REFLECTION OF THAT MAXIM. THE BRICK HEARTH, BUILT WITH ITS OWN SHINGLED ROOF, DOUBLES AS AN OVEN. PINE CABINETS, TILE COUNTERS, AND OPEN SHELVES ADD WARMTH. EVEN THE REFRIGERATOR IS CONCEALED BY A PINE FRONT. THE OLD FARM TABLE HOLDS VINEGAR BOTTLES FILLED WITH HERBS. THE POT RACK MIXES CHILE *RISTRAS* AND GARLIC STRINGS.

ABOVE

DESIGNER PAULA BERG USED THIS CONTEMPORARY KITCHEN
AS A SETTING FOR ANCIENT NATIVE AMERICAN ARTIFACTS. A MARBLE
COUNTERTOP IS ACCENTED BY THE UNUSUAL RANGE HOOD FEATURING OLD
POTTERY SHARDS IN A MOSAIC DESIGN. OPEN SHELVING ALLOWS THE
OWNER TO CHANGE DISPLAYS OFTEN.

RIGHT

AN OPEN, SPACIOUS FEELING MARKS THIS KITCHEN BUILT BY
NANCE CONSTRUCTION. A *SALTILLO* TILE FLOOR BLENDS BEAUTIFULLY
WITH THE RICH WOOD OF THE CABINETS, CENTER ISLAND, AND CEILING
BEAMS. THE STONE MANTEL OUTLINING THE UNUSUAL RANGE HOOD
CREATES SPACE FOR KITCHEN-RELATED DISPLAYS.

OPPOSITE

RICH COBALT BLUE IS A FAVORITE TILE COLOR IN MEXICAN AND
SOUTHWEST KITCHENS, AND THIS ROOM IS ACCENTED BY GEOMETRIC
BORDER MOTIFS IN RED, BLACK, AND WHITE DECORATIVE TILES. THE
ALCOVE IS A UNIQUE SETTING FOR THE STOVE. AN OLD TABLE, PAINTED TO
COMPLEMENT THE TILES, PROVIDES NEEDED WORK SPACE. THE ONCE-OPEN
SINK HAS BEEN ENCLOSED BY BLUE CABINETRY. LOG BEAMS ADD VISUAL
INTEREST TO THE PAINTED CEILING AND SIMPLE LIGHT-BULB CHANDELIER.

ABOVE

THIS KITCHEN AND ADJOINING DINING ROOM ARE A TASTEFUL BLEND OF WESTERN AND VICTORIAN
DESIGN THEMES. THE DARK WOOD OF THE CABINETRY COMPLEMENTS THE RICH HUES OF THE
VICTORIAN FURNISHINGS IN THE DINING ROOM. THE IRONWORK CHANDELIER WITH THE COW MOTIF
LENDS A TOUCH OF HUMOR. AN OLD GROCERY-STORE SCALE ON THE BUTCHER-BLOCK TABLE ADDS
FUNCTIONAL INTEREST.

ABOVE

PAULA BERG USED NEUTRAL SHADES OF WHITE AND GRAY FOR THIS
CONTEMPORARY WESTERN KITCHEN, WITH ITS GRANITE COUNTERTOPS
AND SLATE FLOOR. BAR STOOLS AND DINING CHAIRS FASHIONED OF LOGS
BRING NATURE INDOORS. THE TURQUOISE-LEATHER CHAIR UPHOLSTERY
PROVIDES A SPLASH OF COLOR COMPLEMENTING THE POTTERY. THE
IRONWORK POT RACK OFFERS A PARADE OF BARNYARD ANIMALS—
CHICKENS, DUCKS, COWS, AND GOATS. THE DOORS FROM THE DINING AREA
LEAD TO A DECK, SHOWING MAGNIFICENT SCENERY.

BELOW

DESIGNER NANCY KITCHELL USED A PRIMITIVE AZTEC-STYLE DESIGN IN
THE DECOR OF THIS KITCHEN. NEUTRAL TILE COUNTERTOPS AND
CORRESPONDING CABINETRY BLEND HARMONIOUSLY WITH THE TERRA-
COTTA-COLORED WALLS. THE DECORATIVE LEDGE SHOWCASES ANCIENT
NATIVE AMERICAN ARTIFACTS. AS IN MOST WESTERN KITCHENS, A VIEW
OF NATURE IS ALWAYS CLOSE BY.

LEFT

WARMTH EXUDES FROM THIS KITCHEN, WITH ITS BRICK HEARTH WHERE A POT OF STEW SIMMERS OVER AN OPEN FIRE. HEAVY WOODEN BEAMS COMPLEMENT THE FLOOR AND CABINETRY. THE POT RACK OVERFLOWS WITH COPPER POTS, BASKETS, AND CHILE *RISTRAS*. BLUE-AND-WHITE POTTERY AND UPHOLSTERY ADD A EUROPEAN TOUCH TO THIS INVITING SETTING.

RIGHT

THE KITCHEN IN THIS RESIDENCE IN VICTOR, MONTANA, IS DESIGNED FOR CASUAL LIVING. BOLD LOG BEAMS OF PEELED AND UNPEELED BARK GIVE A MASCULINE INFORMALITY TO THIS AREA OF THE HOME, BUILT BY TIMBERHOUSE POST AND BEAM. WORK SPACES ARE ARRANGED FOR AN EASY FLOW TO THE ADJOINING PLAYROOM.

OPPOSITE

ENTERTAINING IS EASY IN THIS RESIDENCE IN SUN VALLEY, IDAHO. DESIGNER NEIL WRIGHT FASHIONED THE CENTER ISLAND OF PINE SO THAT IT WOULD DOUBLE AS A BAR AND WORK SPACE. GUESTS CAN VISIT WITH THE CHEF WHILE DINNER IS BEING PREPARED OR HOVER AROUND THE STONE FIREPLACE FOR CONVERSATION.

ABOVE

TWILIGHT IS A SPECIAL TIME IN THIS LOG HOME IN BIGFORK, MONTANA, BUILT BY ROCKY MOUNTAIN HABITATS AND DESIGNED BY GARY KAUFMAN. PUNCHED-TIN HANGING LAMPS DEFINE THE SHAPE OF THE KITCHEN SERVING COUNTER AND ALSO CREATE A VISUAL BREAK BETWEEN THE KITCHEN AND THE FAMILY ROOM. A ROCK FIREPLACE IS A COZY SPOT FOR FRIENDS AND FAMILY TO GATHER.

ABOVE

A FEELING OF OPENNESS MARKS THE SPACIOUS AND FUNCTIONAL KITCHEN IN
THIS RESIDENCE IN COLUMBIA FALLS, MONTANA. CABINETS AND COUNTERTOPS
DESIGNED BY SHIMO CABINETS FEATURE WHITE-PORCELAIN KNOBS AND MIX OPEN
AND CLOSED SHELVING, ALLOWING THE FAMILY TO DISPLAY A VARIETY OF COLLECTIBLES.
OVAL AND HEART-SHAPED BRAIDED RUGS ACCENT THE PLANK FLOORING.

ABOVE

ARCHITECT JON SAYLER MADE WOOD THE STAR IN THIS PRIEST LAKE, IDAHO, KITCHEN. LOGS FORMING THE CEILING AND SUPPORT BEAMS HAVE A RICH PATINA, AS DO THE CHAIRS LINING THE SERVING BAR. GLASS SHELVES DISPLAY FAVORITE DISHES, WHILE THE WOOD-GRAIN COUNTERTOP IS ACCENTED BY A COLLECTION OF BRIGHTLY COLORED POTTERY JARS.

BELOW

THE SERVING BAR IN THIS KITCHEN PROVIDES AN EASY PLACE FOR THE FAMILY TO GATHER FOR INFORMAL DINING. THE BLUE-AND-GRAY-TILE COUNTERTOP CONTRASTS THE CABINETRY. THE ABSENCE OF DRAPERIES, TYPICAL OF WESTERN DECOR, MAKES NATURE A CONSTANT COMPANION IN THIS SETTING.

BELOW

WHITEWASHED LOGS CREATE AN INTERESTING CEILING PATTERN IN THIS CONTEMPORARY HOME IN VAIL, COLORADO, DESIGNED BY ALPINE LOG HOMES. A CENTER-ISLAND STORAGE AND WORK SPACE IS THE FUNCTIONAL HUB OF THE KITCHEN. COPPER POTS AND UTENSILS DECORATE THE CEILING, AS DOES AN ASSORTMENT OF OTHER COLLECTIBLES.

ABOVE

ENTERTAINING IS A JOY IN THIS MONTANA RESIDENCE. ARCHITECT JERRY LOCATI DESIGNED THE HOME FOR A GOOD TRAFFIC FLOW FROM KITCHEN TO ADJOINING DINING AND FAMILY ROOMS. IN COLOR AND TEXTURE, THE GRANITE COUNTERTOP IS A FOIL TO THE CHARMINGLY RUSTIC ROCK FIREPLACE AND LOG WALLS AND BEAMS. THE DESIGN IS BY KENT INTERIORS, WITH CABINETRY BY MCPHIE.

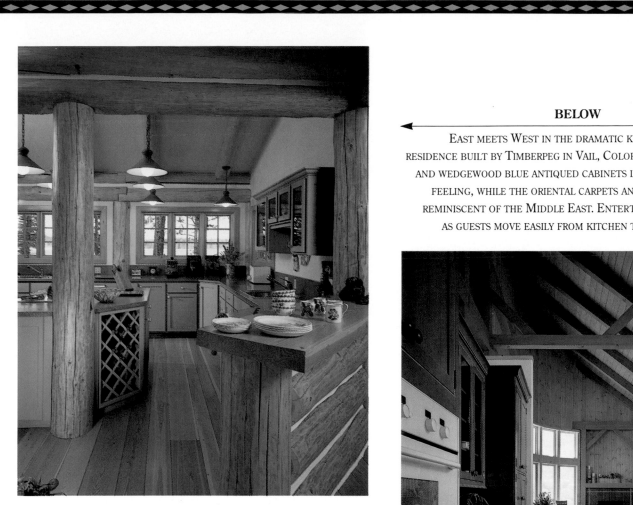

BELOW

EAST MEETS WEST IN THE DRAMATIC KITCHEN OF THIS
RESIDENCE BUILT BY TIMBERPEG IN VAIL, COLORADO. THE PINE TIMBERS
AND WEDGEWOOD BLUE ANTIQUED CABINETS LEND A NEW ENGLAND
FEELING, WHILE THE ORIENTAL CARPETS AND UPHOLSTERY ARE
REMINISCENT OF THE MIDDLE EAST. ENTERTAINING IS INFORMAL,
AS GUESTS MOVE EASILY FROM KITCHEN TO FAMILY ROOM.

ABOVE

A CONTEMPORARY OPEN-AIR FEELING WAS CREATED IN THE KITCHEN
BY ARCHITECT JEAN STEINBRECHER AND LACHANCE BUILDERS FOR THIS
RESIDENCE IN WHITEFISH, MONTANA. THE DIAGONAL BARS AND WORK
SPACES LEND ARCHITECTURAL APPEAL TO THE HORIZONTAL SHAPE OF THE
ROOM. THE DEEP TURQUOISE CABINETRY ADDS SPICE TO THE LOG-AND-
MORTAR INTERIOR.

OPPOSITE

WESTERN WEDS FRENCH COUNTRY IN THIS HOME IN MCCALL, IDAHO,
BUILT BY ARCHITECT KEVIN MCKEE AND GARLAND LOG HOMES. ROUGH
CEDAR LOGS, A DARK WOOD FLOOR, AND ROCK TRIM AT THE CEILING ARE
MASCULINE TOUCHES; THE DELICATE TILE MOTIF IN THE RANGE HOOD AND
SKYLIGHT ADDS FEMININE CHARM. INTERIOR DESIGN IS BY WARREN SHEETS.

LEFT

DINING FOR TWO IS A DELIGHT IN THIS RESIDENCE IN WHITEFISH, MONTANA, BUILT BY TIMBERPEG. THE CENTER-ISLAND WORK SPACE AND WINE RACK ARE FOCAL POINTS IN THE PINE-PANELED KITCHEN AND ADJACENT DINING AREA. GUESTS ARE SEATED IN TWIG CHAIRS WITH TALL REEDLIKE BRANCHES THAT ECHO BRANCHES OUTSIDE. A NAVAJO BLANKET SERVES AS A TABLE SKIRT.

ABOVE

SUBSTANTIAL BUT COZY IS THE FEELING IN THIS HOME THAT PRESENTS A VARIETY OF WESTERN
DESIGN THEMES. LARGE TIMBER BEAMS AND SUPPORT POSTS ARE ENHANCED BY CERAMIC-TILE
COUNTERTOPS, PINE CABINETS, AND BRICK FIREPLACE AND STOVE. ANTIQUE FURNISHINGS AND
PLUSH UPHOLSTERY ADD A COMFORTABLE LOOK. LONG VERTICAL WINDOWS MAKE THE GARDEN AN
INTEGRAL PART OF THE ROOM.

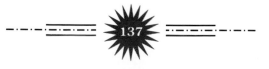

ABOVE

COMPACT SPACES MARK THE SAME RESIDENCE IN BIGFORK, MONTANA, DESIGNED BY ARCHITECT JERRY LOCATI. THE RICH COLOR OF CEDAR CONTRASTS THE BLACK COUNTERTOP AND SMOKE SHADES ON THE LIGHTING FIXTURES. DECORATIVE MOLDING AND RECESSED LIGHTING ADD VISUAL INTEREST TO THE CEILING. THE L-SHAPED WORK ISLAND IS AN IDEAL PLACE FOR AN INFORMAL REPAST.

ABOVE

AN EXPANSIVE INTERIOR VIEW OF THIS RESIDENCE REVEALS HOW BEAUTIFULLY THE SPACE WORKS FOR ENTERTAINING, INDOORS OR OUT. THE HIGH CEILING AND PLACEMENT OF CROSS TIMBERS LEND A LODGE FEELING TO THE ROOM. THE DINING CHAIRS AND TABLE SUGGEST THE INFLUENCE OF FRANK LLOYD WRIGHT AND GUSTAV STICKLEY.

THIS VIEW OF THE SAME RESIDENCE SHOWS HOW WELL THE CABINETRY BY MCPHIE WORKS TO PROVIDE BEAUTY AND FUNCTION. THE ARCHITECT ALSO DESIGNED THE OPEN SPACES ABOVE THE SUPPORT BEAMS TO SHOWCASE SOME OF THE FAMILY'S UNUSUAL COLLECTIBLES.

ABOVE

A TOUCH OF FRANK LLOYD WRIGHT INFLUENCE IS SEEN IN THIS RESIDENCE IN BIG SKY, MONTANA. ARCHITECT JAMES D. MORTON MIXED HORIZONTAL AND VERTICAL LINES WITH PYRAMID SHAPES TO CREATE THIS SPACIOUS, WELL-APPOINTED KITCHEN AND ADJACENT FAMILY ROOM. THE WARMTH OF CEDAR WOOD IS COMPLEMENTED BY THE LUSH PINES OUTDOORS.

BELOW

THE SMALL, COMPACT, AND FUNCTIONAL SPACE MAKES THE KITCHEN AN EASY PLACE TO COOK. A COPPER RANGE HOOD IS ECHOED IN THE FAMILY'S COLLECTION OF COPPER UTENSILS. HANGING CEILING LIGHTS HERE AND ABOVE THE DINING TABLE IN ANOTHER VIEW ARE STRONGLY REMINISCENT OF ART DECO AND ART NOUVEAU DESIGN.

ABOVE

A CONTEMPORARY PAINTING OF COWBOYS HANGS ABOVE THE FIREPLACE IN THE SEATING AREA OFF THE DINING ROOM AND KITCHEN OF THIS HOME. WOOD PANELING IS A MAJOR FOCAL POINT, AS IS THE CHECKERBOARD DESIGN OF THE TILE FLOOR, A PATTERN REPEATED IN THE GRAY, SAND, AND WHITE UPHOLSTERY.

OPPOSITE

FRANK LLOYD WRIGHT AND GUSTAV STICKLEY WOULD HAVE FELT RIGHT AT HOME AT THIS DINING TABLE WITH CHAIRS INSPIRED BY THEIR MODERNISTIC DESIGNS. CREAMY WALLS ACCENTED BY CROWN MOLDINGS, TILE FLOORS, MARBLE COUNTERTOPS, AND MAHOGANY CABINETS AND SHELVING MAKE THIS AN INVITING HOME IN THE WESTERN STYLE.

ABOVE

LEFT: AN UNUSUAL MÉLANGE OF ANGLES, FROM CURVING AND RECTANGULAR TO VERTICAL AND HORIZONTAL, CHARACTERIZE THIS KITCHEN. IN THE FOREGROUND, AN ANTIQUE DROP-LEAF TABLE IS THE PERFECT PLACE FOR COFFEE OR SMALL MEALS. THE CHAIRS, WITH THEIR BLUE LEATHER SEATS AND YELLOW BACKS, ADD A DASH OF MODERNISTIC FUN TO A TRADITIONAL SETTING. *RIGHT:* A RICH, DARK YELLOW STAIN WAS CHOSEN TO HIGHLIGHT AND BEAUTIFY THE CABINETS. THE COUNTERTOP BACKSPLASH FEATURES AN UNUSUAL DEEP BROWN MARBLE EFFECT.

OPPOSITE

THE MOOD OF A MEXICAN *HACIENDA* IS EVIDENT IN THIS DRAMATIC SETTING. STARK WHITE WALLS GIVE MORE PROMINENCE TO THE PERIWINKLE BLUE KITCHEN WALL. CEILING TIMBERS AND CLERESTORY WINDOWS ADD ARCHITECTURAL INTEREST. THE PLAIN TILE FLOOR, CONTRASTED BY THE LEATHER-COVERED TABLE AND BASKET CHAIRS, STONEWARE JARS, AND DARK BROWN BOWLS ON THE BAKER'S RACK, POINTS THE WAY TO THE KITCHEN.

LIVING ROOMS

HAVENS OF COMFORT

Living rooms—or *salas*—of the West are conspicuous in their absence of draperies. When nature has painted such beautiful portraits for all to enjoy, there seems no need for camouflage. Windows that reveal eye-catching vistas—views that stretch the imagination as much as they please the eye—are often the starting point for a living room's interior design.

But if there *are* draperies, you can bet your boots they'll be stitched with leather or buckskin or adorned with fringe or beads. Even the rods will be of wrought iron, maybe employing a cowboys-and-Indians motif. Canvas, ticking, lace, and plantation shutters are other Western-design alternatives.

After one has decided to drape (or not to drape), the fireplace is the next consideration. No living room that adopts a Western-style design would be complete without a fireplace and the obligatory pinion woods. Fashioned of rock, native stone, or adobe, it always dominates the room, as if making a bold statement about its importance. Old andirons, utensils, and cast-iron kettles are reminders of a fireplace's utilitarian heritage. Hearth mantels often display everything from rustic pottery and baskets to framed ancestral mementos. And always, those venerable trophies and trappings of the hunt—mooseheads, elkhorn antlers,

ABOVE: THE LIVING ROOM OF SCULPTOR JOHN MORTENSEN'S HOME BLENDS RUSTIC AND TRADITIONAL THEMES. *OPPOSITE:* THIS LIVING ROOM EXUDES SOUTHWEST STYLE AND WESTERN HOSPITALITY.

and fishing creels—show to advantage over the fireplace.

One major piece—perhaps a favorite antique—will often dominate the living room. It could be a leather-covered burl pedestal table, keyhole or gunfighter chairs, a deer-antler chandelier, or an armoire with painted panels that tell a special story of the West.

In living rooms, art can range from turn-of-the-century to contemporary, but it is almost always showcased against wood paneling, logs, or brick. A profusion of plants brings nature inside, complementing the larger theater of the often spectacular surrounding landscape.

Whether the furnishings are fashioned of Mexican Colonial leather, Molesworth-inspired reproductions upholstered in Navajo weavings, or simple pine covered in sturdy denim or canvas, a living room decorated Western style always exudes comfort and charm. It easily harks back to a time when cowboys and ranchers lived a more unfettered existence.

ABOVE

CURLING UP BESIDE THE FIRE IS SPECIAL IN THIS UNUSUAL SANTA FE HOME. *BANCOS* LINE THE ADOBE FIREPLACE, ACCENTED WITH CUSHIONS AND PILLOWS IN BRIGHT COLORS COMPLEMENTING THE ORIENTAL RUG. THE *BANCOS* ALSO SERVE AS STORAGE PLACES FOR LOGS AND FIREPLACE ACCESSORIES. *NICHOS* DISPLAY *SANTOS* AND CROSSES, WHILE WEAVINGS ADORN THE WALLS.

LEFT

WHAT BETTER PLACE FOR COFFEE THAN IN FRONT OF A COZY ADOBE FIREPLACE? RATTAN CHAIRS SIDLE UP TO A CLEVER MEXICAN FOLK-ART TABLE, TOPPED WITH GLASS FOR EASY ENTERTAINING. LARGE WROUGHT-IRON CANDLEHOLDERS ADD THEIR OWN GLOW TO THIS SETTING, WHICH FEATURES MINIMAL DECORATING AND MAXIMUM ARCHITECTURAL IMPACT.

OPPOSITE

FOLK ART AND BASKETS ARE USED SPARINGLY TO ACCESSORIZE THIS FIREPLACE. A WOVEN BASKET HOLDS LOGS, WHILE OTHERS DRESS THE WALL AND SMALL MANTEL. THE FOLK-ART FIGURE OF ST. FRANCIS OF ASSISI IS A POPULAR SOUTHWEST ICON.

LEFT

All eyes are cast upward at the unusual arched wood ceiling with its bricklike appearance. Julia Tometz's design is compatible with the ceiling *vigas* and *corbels* in the living room. Subtle hallway lighting mixes cultures: oriental, as seen in the Tansu chest, and *nichos* for presenting Native American artifacts.

OPPOSITE

Julia Tometz created a masterful mix of styles and textures in this living room dominated by the fireplace. The upholstered settees are angled, while other furnishings, particularly the ironwork sofa and *latilla* screen, complement the design. The marble table, which reflects the carpet pattern, rests on a flagstone floor.

ABOVE

MOORISH, SPANISH, MEXICAN, AND ORIENTAL INFLUENCES ARE
EXPRESSED IN THIS FIREPLACE DESIGN. OLD-WORLD CATHEDRAL DETAILING
IS SHOWN IN THE ORNATE STONEWORK, BY NANCE CONSTRUCTION. THE
SCREEN REPEATS THE CIRCULAR MOTIFS IN THE FIREPLACE DETAILING AND
THE ARCHWAYS. THE TIN MIRROR, ORIENTAL CARPET, OLD WOODEN CHEST,
AND TERRA COTTA POTS FURTHER THE MULTICULTURAL MOOD.

BELOW

A SIMPLE ADOBE ARCHWAY BECOMES A WORK OF ART IN THIS SOUTHWEST
HOME. A *TROMPE L'OEIL* EFFECT IS ACHIEVED WITH THE DELICATE BLUE,
RED, AND GOLD PATTERN CREATING FAUX BALUSTRADES AND A CURVING
DESIGN THAT ACCENTS THE ENTRY TO THE INFORMAL LIVING ROOM. OLD
DRUMS AND A GUITAR FLANK THE SOFA.

ABOVE

THE RICH PURPLE OF A SOUTHWEST SUNSET IS A MAGNIFICENT CONTRAST TO THE NEUTRAL DECOR DESIGNED BY NANCY KITCHELL. ADOBE WALLS ARE ACCENTED BY THE LIGHT WOOD TREATMENT ON THE FIREPLACE AND CABINETRY. MOSAIC UPHOLSTERY AND TAPESTRY COLORS ADD MOORISH INFLUENCES, AS DOES THE FIREPLACE MIRROR.

ARCHITECT JOHN MCMAHON USED SQUARES AND RECTANGLES FOR THE DESIGN OF HIS HOME. THE THEME IS REPEATED IN THE SHAPES OF THE FIREPLACE AND WROUGHT-IRON COFFEE TABLE. MIMINAL COLOR IS ADDED TO THE NEUTRAL SETTING, WHICH HAS AN AIRY, OPEN FEELING.

ABOVE

SIMPLICITY OF DESIGN MARKS THIS HOUSE, BY THE ARCHITECTURAL FIRM OF MARROW, BOWDEN. RICHLY STAINED WOOD-BEAM CEILINGS AND DOORS CONTRAST THE PRISTINE, WHITE-STUCCO WALLS. BLACK-LEATHER SOFAS ARE ACCENTED WITH PILLOWS COVERED IN NAVAJO WEAVING. DRUMS BEAT OUT A FUNCTIONAL MESSAGE WHEN SERVING AS COFFEE AND END TABLES. CARVED INDIAN DANCERS USE THE DRUM AS THEIR STAGE.

ABOVE

STREAMLINED ORIENTAL ARCHITECTURAL THEMES SEEM TO BLEND WITH SUBTLE SOUTHWEST
DESIGN ELEMENTS IN THIS HOUSE. NEUTRAL WALLS AND SPARE ORNAMENTATION MAKE THE
ARCHITECTURAL ANGLES AND CLERESTORY WINDOWS MORE DRAMATIC. FURNISHINGS, CABINETRY,
AND STORAGE CHESTS LEND HORIZONTAL SHAPES, AS DO THE WALL INSETS FOR ARTIFACTS.
AN ANCIENT ARCHITECTURAL COLUMN GREETS VISITORS IN THE TILE ENTRYWAY.

ABOVE

DESIGNER MELINDA RYERSON USED THE MAGNIFICENT BLUES, GREENS, ORANGES, AND
PURPLES OF NATURE IN THE SOFA, PILLOWS, AND THROWS OF THIS SOUTHWEST LIVING ROOM. AN
UNUSUAL CURVED STONE TABLE WITH A ROCK-LEDGE SHELF FLANKS THE SOFA AND IS A PERFECT
SURFACE FOR BASKETRY AND METALWORK LAMPS.

ABOVE

ARCHITECT ED FITZGERALD CHOSE A THOROUGHLY MODERN, LINEAR THEME FOR THIS
WESTERN-STYLE HOME. BLACK-AND-WHITE TILE AND CABINETRY HARMONIZE WITH THE PINE-PLANK
FLOORING, THE FLOOR-TO-CEILING WINDOWS, STREAMLINED IRON RAILINGS INSIDE AND OUT, AND
RECESSED LIGHTING. FURNISHINGS ARE MINIMAL, WITH LEATHER WASSILY CHAIRS COMPLEMENTING
THE STEEL-AND-GLASS COFFEE TABLE.

ABOVE

THIS RESIDENCE EXPRESSES A SLEEK ARCHITECTURAL THEME.

OPPOSITE

THE LIVING ROOM OF THIS HOME IN RANCHO MIRAGE SUGGESTS A TYPICAL SERENE,
OFF-WHITE DESIGN THEME FAVORED BY CALIFORNIA DESIGNERS.

LEFT

CHROME AND GLASS WERE ONCE THE
ANTITHESIS OF WESTERN DESIGN. BUT WHEN
THEY ARE INCORPORATED IN A WIDE-OPEN
DESIGN SUCH AS THIS ONE, WITH THE
GLEAMING FINISH OF THE WOOD FLOORS AND
STAIRWAY, A WHITE-STUCCO INTERIOR, AND
JEWEL-TONE HUES IN THE UPHOLSTERY AND
CARPETS, THE LOOK CAN SEEM RIGHT AT
HOME IN THE WEST.

OPPOSITE

WHEN THE ARCHITECTURAL DESIGN OF A
HOME IS SO SPECTACULAR, THERE'S LITTLE
NEED FOR EXTRANEOUS ORNAMENTATION.
"LONG, LEAN, AND LINEAR" IS AN APT
DESCRIPTION FOR THIS LIVING AREA, WHICH
FEATURES SIMPLE LINES IN THE FURNISHINGS
AND NEUTRAL UPHOLSTERY. THE EXPANSIVE
WINDOWS OFFER A VIEW OF THE POOL AND
ADJOINING PATIO.

OPPOSITE

WOOD, LEATHER, AND NATURE BLEND HARMONIOUSLY IN THIS HOME, WHICH FEATURES CLEAN, SIMPLE LINES IN ITS ARCHITECTURE, MARKED BY UNUSUAL WINDOW AND CEILING TREATMENTS. THE BOLD TILE FLOORS ADD A TEXTURAL CONTRAST TO THE LEATHER SOFAS FLANKING AN OLD WOODEN PLANK TABLE. THE OVERSIZE TAPESTRY PILLOWS AND ANTIQUE CHAIR SUGGEST A MIDDLE EASTERN INFLUENCE.

ABOVE

ARTIST ED MELL CALLS THIS COZY SETTING HOME. EARLY-DAY FURNISHINGS SPORT NAVAJO WEAVINGS IN THE UPHOLSTERY, WITH CONTRAST OFFERED BY AN ORIENTAL CARPET ON PINE-PLANK FLOORS. A LOFT OVERLOOKS THE SETTING, WHILE NATURE IS READILY AVAILABLE TO PAINT FROM THE ARTIST'S VIEW ON THE DECK.

RIGHT

WHAT BETTER PLACE FOR AN ARTIST TO PONDER HIS LATEST INSPIRATION OR READ BOOKS ABOUT HIS ARTISTIC IDOLS THAN IN FRONT OF A FIREPLACE? THE CONCRETE BLOCKS SUGGEST A RUSTIC SIMPLICITY, AS DOES THE SIMPLE MANTEL, DISPLAYING A KACHINA DOLL, AN ACOMA POT, A WESTERN SCULPTURE, AND THE WEST'S FAVORITE BOUQUET, BRIGHT SUNFLOWERS.

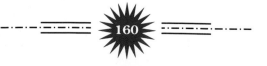

ABOVE

WOOD TIMBERS DOMINATE THE SCENE IN THIS RESIDENCE, AND THIS VIEW SHOWS HOW WELL THE LIVING ROOM AND DINING ROOM WORK TOGETHER FOR ENTERTAINING. THE UNUSUAL WEDGEWOOD-BLUE CHINA CABINET CONTRASTS THE PINE WALLS, REPEATING THE SUBTLE COLOR SCHEME IN THE UPHOLSTERY. AN OLD DOOR MAKES A CLEVER COFFEE TABLE.

BELOW

THE VIEW INSIDE THE SAME VAIL, COLORADO, HOME IS JUST AS ARCHITECTURALLY EXCITING AS IT IS IN NATURE'S THEATER. A MEDLEY OF CRISS-CROSSING TIMBERS OFFERS VISUAL INTEREST IN THE DINING AND LIVING ROOM AREA, WITH EXPANSIVE SKYLIGHTS PROVIDING ANOTHER WAY TO BRING NATURE INDOORS. THE DINING ROOM FURNITURE REFLECTS EARLY MISSION-STYLE INFLUENCES.

ABOVE

WHEN THIS FAMILY ENTERTAINS, THE PATIO IS A PERFECT SETTING. HERE, GUESTS NOT
ONLY ENJOY THE VIEW THAT NATURE HAS PROVIDED WITH ROCK BOULDERS AND WALLS, BUT ALSO
THE ARCHITECTURAL SCENE CREATED BY TIMBERPEG WITH ITS UNUSUAL WOOD-AND-STUCCO DESIGN
EMPLOYING VARIOUS GEOMETRIC ANGLES.

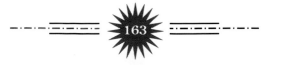

ARCHITECT JERRY LOCATI BLENDED WESTERN DESIGN ELEMENTS FOR THE SAME LIVING ROOM IN BIGFORK, MONTANA. WINDOWS PROVIDE AN EXCELLENT VIEW OF THE MOUNTAINS, LAKE, AND TALL TIMBERS INDIGENOUS TO THIS PART OF THE WEST. EXPOSED BEAMS, ROCK WALLS, AND STURDY FURNISHINGS UPHOLSTERED IN LEATHER AND NAVAJO MOTIFS LEAVE NO DOUBT THAT THE HOMEOWNERS LOVE THE WEST.

ABOVE

THIS LIVING ROOM, DESIGNED BY KENT INTERIORS, HAS THE FEELING OF AN OLD LODGE, WITH THE MASSIVE STONE FIREPLACE AND THE HEAVY TIMBERS OF THE CEILING BEAMS. THE EFFECT OF THE SPLIT MANTEL, PAINTED WHITE FOR CONTRAST, MAKES CHANGING DISPLAYS VISUALLY INTERESTING FOR GUESTS.

ABOVE

IMAGINE A FAMILY GATHERED AROUND THE PIANO TO SING OLD WESTERN TUNES WITH
FRIENDS AND RELATIVES. THIS ROOM SPELLS WARMTH AND COMFORT, WITH ITS BLAZING HEARTH
AND INVITING CHAIRS AND SOFAS. NATIVE AMERICAN UPHOLSTERY AND A MEXICAN
SERAPE COVERING THE COFFEE TABLE SHOW HOW WELL CULTURAL STYLES CAN BLEND.

CAN TRADITIONAL FURNISHINGS FIND
A HAPPY HOME IN THE WEST? THIS
RESIDENCE IN HELENA, MONTANA, BUILT BY
TIMBERHOUSE, SUGGESTS A WELL-PLANNED
MARRIAGE OF ARCHITECTURAL AND INTERIOR-
DESIGN STYLES. THE HEAVY ARCHED TIMBERS
COMPLEMENT THE TALL VERTICAL WINDOW
WITH ITS MAGNIFICENT VIEW. VICTORIAN AND
TRADITIONAL FURNISHINGS AND ACCESSORIES
LEND ELEGANCE.

OPPOSITE

NO PLACE TO STORE YOUR SNOW SKIS?
THEN HANG THEM ON THE WALL AS A
DECORATIVE TOUCH. THAT'S ONE OF THE
FOCAL POINTS IN THIS COMFORTABLE LIVING
ROOM, DECORATED WITH A COWBOYS-AND-
INDIANS THEME. COWHIDE UPHOLSTERY
BLENDS WITH NATIVE AMERICAN PILLOWS
AND SEAT CUSHIONS, WHILE A PATCHWORK
OTTOMAN, FLORAL DRAPERIES, AND AN
ORIENTAL RUG ADD OLD-FASHIONED CHARM.

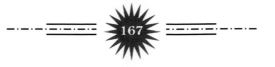

INTERIOR DESIGN

BELOW

THE EARLY PIONEERS WHO SETTLED THE WEST AND LIVED IN PRIMITIVE LOG CABINS WOULD SURELY COVET THIS LOG HOME IN MONTANA, BY ARCHITECT PHIL KORELL. MASSIVE LOGS AND CEILING TIMBERS ENHANCE THE ROUGH STONE FIREPLACE AND CURVING WHITE MANTEL, WHICH DISPLAYS BASKETS AND ANIMAL SCULPTURES. THE OPEN TIMBERS REVEAL OWLS AND A DEER HEAD.

ABOVE

A NATIVE AMERICAN INTERIOR-DESIGN THEME BLENDS WELL WITH THE UPDATED LOG-CABIN LOOK IN THIS MOUNTAIN HIDEAWAY BY ALPINE LOG HOMES. THE BOLD STUCCO FIREPLACE, WITH ITS HANDSOME STUFFED DEER HEAD AND FIVE-POINT ANTLERS, HIGHLIGHTS THE LOG-AND-MORTAR CONSTRUCTION. THE BRICK HEARTH AND ADIRONDACK-STYLE TABLES ARE OTHER RUSTIC DESIGN TOUCHES.

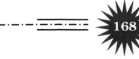

ABOVE

CUSTOM LOG HOMES USED STACKED STONE, PINE FLOORS, AND AND LOGS FOR THIS LIVING ROOM IN JACKSON HOLE, WYOMING. THE ORANGE-LEATHER SOFA PICKS UP THE COLORS IN THE ORIENTAL AND NAVAJO RUGS. AN OLD WOODEN BOARD IS RECYCLED AS A COFFEE TABLE. WARM THROWS AND AN ABUNDANCE OF BOOKS BECKON THE FAMILY TO ENJOY COMFORTABLE AFTERNOONS AND EVENINGS AROUND A ROARING FIRE.

BELOW

FOR THIS STEAMBOAT SPRINGS, COLORADO, HOME, MONTANA LOG HOMES USED ROCK, TILE, AND LOGS TO ACHIEVE A RUSTIC EFFECT. THE TWO-STORY ROCK FIREPLACE ANCHORS THE ROOM, WITH ITS SCREEN ADDING ANOTHER VIEW OF THE WEST. LEATHER FURNISHINGS, SIMPLE WOOD TABLES, BALCONY, AND SKYLIGHTS MAKE A STATEMENT ABOUT THE IMPORTANCE OF COMFORT.

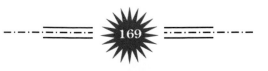

ABOVE

THE UNUSUAL ENTRYWAY OF THIS RESIDENCE
IS DIVIDED BY TWO GRAND STAIRCASES
LEADING TO UPSTAIRS BEDROOMS. THE
CLERESTORY WINDOWS AND WALL SCONCES
ARE OTHER DELIGHTFUL DETAILS, AS ARE THE
SEVERAL CONVERSATIONAL AREAS, COWHIDE
PILLOWS, AND UNUSUAL TWIG CHAIRS
REMINISCENT OF THE BENTWOOD STYLE.

ABOVE

THIS VIEW OF A MAGNIFICENT LOG HOME, DESIGNED BY ALPINE LOG HOMES, SHOWS HOW WELL
CONVERSATIONAL AREAS ARE DIVIDED BY A TABLE AND CONTEMPORARY WOOD LAMPS. A SMALL
ALCOVE DOUBLES AS A GUEST ROOM OR LIBRARY. THE BLEACHED LOGS MAKE AN ATTRACTIVE
RAILING FOR DISPLAYING PENDLETON BLANKETS.

ABOVE

ONE SUSPECTS ARCHITECT JERRY LOCATI GREW UP PLAYING WITH TINKER TOYS AND NEVER OUTGREW HIS FASCINATION WITH CREATING BEAUTIFUL LOG DWELLINGS. THIS VIEW OF THE SAME RESIDENCE REVEALS HOW WARM AND COMFORTING LOG HOMES CAN BE. LEATHER FURNISHINGS, NAVAJO BLANKETS, AND VARIOUS ARTIFACTS MAKE THIS A VISUALLY EXCITING ROOM.

ABOVE

IN THIS MONTANA HOME, ROCKS MAKE A DRAMATIC STATEMENT IN FIREPLACES AND STONE PILLARS. NAVAJO RUGS SERVE AS UPHOLSTERY, AND IN THE LEATHER-COVERED SEATING AREA THE COFFEE TABLE RESEMBLES AN OLD SLED. THE HANGING ARTIFACT SUGGESTS NORTHWEST COAST INDIAN INFLUENCES.

ABOVE

ANIMAL SCULPTURES PRANCE ACROSS THE STONE FIREPLACE IN THIS RESIDENCE IN WHITEFISH,
MONTANA, AND ARE REPEATED IN THE METAL LAMP NEAR THE SOFA. PLAID WINGBACK CHAIRS
BLEND WELL WITH THE RED-LEATHER CHAIR AND UPHOLSTERED SOFA.

OPPOSITE

THE MAIN SEATING AREA AT KOOTENAI LODGE IN SWAN LAKE, MONTANA, EASILY TAKES GUESTS
BACK TO THE DAYS WHEN RAILROADS BUILT LODGES IN WYOMING AND MONTANA.

ABOVE

A STACKED-STONE FIREPLACE AND ADJOINING LEDGE DIVIDE THIS LIVING ROOM AND ELEVATED DINING AREA. STAIRS BEHIND THE FIREPLACE AND TO THE RIGHT OF THE LEDGE LEAD TO THE DINING AREA. SILK-AND-LINEN-UPHOLSTERED SOFAS, LEATHER CHAIRS, AND ORIENTAL CARPETS REFLECT TRADITIONAL THEMES. CONTRAST IS ADDED WITH THE PRIMITIVE COFFEE TABLE, ANCIENT FIGURES BY THE FIREPLACE, AND CONTEMPORARY PAINTINGS.

LEFT

THIS LIVING ROOM COULD EASILY BE IN ANY PART OF THE UNITED STATES, WERE IT NOT FOR THE WHITE-ADOBE BRICKS AND THE DARK PINE BEAMS ACCENTING THE PLANK CEILING. INSTEAD, IT WAS DESIGNED BY CCBC, INC., FOR A WICKENBURG, ARIZONA, RESIDENCE. A GRAY-STONE FIREPLACE WITH A SHELL PEDIMENT ADDS ARCHITECTURAL INTEREST TO THE RICH SALMON-AND-GREEN COLOR SCHEME OF UPHOLSTERY AND DRAPES.

LEFT

Designer Charles Stuhlberg used two white sofas in the living area of this residence in Sun Valley, Idaho, to contrast the ceiling's dark wood timbers. The rich plank flooring and massive stone wall separate the living area from the kitchen. A traditional Navajo rug and blue, red, and white accents in pillows and upholstery lend a traditional feeling to this Western-style home.

OPPOSITE

Rich terra cotta adobe walls add a dramatic warmth to this contemporary setting designed by Nancy Kitchell. Middle Eastern and Mediterranean design themes are used in the textured upholstery. The coffee table has a woven-leather base and beveled-glass top, on which sits a striking stone vase. Note the unusual masklike sculptures made from humble garden tools.

DINING ROOMS

STAGES FOR STORYTELLING

Listen closely as you sit around the dining tables of the West, and you can just about imagine the spirited tall tales that once were told and whispered. In earlier times, such stories, whether based in fact or in fancy, would have been related around the campfire as cowboys ate hearty chuck-wagon fare—beef stew, sourdough biscuits, peach cobbler, and strong black coffee.

Western-style dining rooms—or *comedores*—invite convivial informality. They are where families and friends share the events of the day, sampling simple fare and the joys of homespun friendship and camaraderie.

The table is the centerpiece of this all-important room. It can be a 19th-century Welsh country table, a zinc-topped Rustic-style table, a restored Art Deco treasure, a thick sheet of glass topping a burled-wood base, or a traditional trestle table. Flanking the table will be leather chairs studded

ABOVE: A LONG HARVEST TABLE, ACCENTED BY AN OLD WAGON-WHEEL-AND-LANTERN CHANDELIER, IS THE CENTERPIECE OF THE DINING ROOM IN THIS PALM SPRINGS, CALIFORNIA, HOME. *OPPOSITE:* OLD-FASHIONED WESTERN HOSPITALITY ABOUNDS IN THIS RUSTIC HOME, WITH ITS PANELED WALLS, PLANK CEILING, AND SUPPORTING TIMBERS.

with nailheads, or ladder backs with cane seats, or rabbit-ear chairs dressed in cowhide or gingham. Old park benches and church pews, like many other elements of Western design, enjoy a new use tableside. Almost always, a patterned rug—an oriental or dhurrie or kilim—adds texture and color under the table.

A staghorn or wagonwheel chandelier hovers overhead. A hand-stenciled border encircles the ceiling. Adorning the table is a centerpiece. It can be dried or fresh flowers, beeswax candles in wrought iron or ceramic candleholders, or an unusual piece of sculpture. The table may be set with imported china, cowboy collectibles, or Fiestaware. Napkins may be the finest linen or simple red bandannas. Silver and crystal will also reflect the family's style of entertaining.

But always at the heart of the room is the meal itself—perfectly seasoned, whether it's spicy Southwest or California nouvelle cuisine.

ABOVE

A TRUE SOUTHWEST SPIRIT IS REFLECTED IN THIS DINING ROOM THAT MIXES CONTEMPORARY ARCHITECTURAL THEMES WITH RUSTIC-STYLE FURNISHINGS AND COWBOY ART ABOVE THE SERVING CREDENZA. NOTE THE SUN-GOD MOTIF OF THE HAND-CARVED CHAIRS.

OPPOSITE

THE OWNERS OF THIS JACKSON HOLE, WYOMING, HOME CAN OBSERVE THE GRAND TETONS' BREATHTAKING BEAUTY FROM THEIR DINING AREA'S EXPANSIVE WINDOWS.

BELOW

COWBOYS AND INDIANS ARE PERPETUAL GUESTS AT THIS DINING-ROOM TABLE IN KETCHUM, IDAHO, AS THEY CIRCLE THE BASE OF THE UNUSUAL METAL-AND-GLASS CHANDELIER. HEAVY LOG BEAMS ALSO SERVE AS A SHOWPLACE FOR NAVAJO RUGS AND BLANKETS. LOG CHAIRS AND OTHER FURNISHINGS REST ON ORIENTAL CARPETS.

ABOVE

THE HOMEOWNERS WANTED A LOG CABIN IN THE WOODS OF WHITEFISH, MONTANA. BUT WHAT OLD STYLE LOG WORKS AND LACHANCE BUILDERS BUILT IS DEFINITELY AN UPSCALE VERSION. LOG BEAMS ADD ARCHITECTURAL INTEREST IN THE KITCHEN, DINING AREA, AND LIVING ROOM; THEY'RE ALSO FUNCTIONAL, WHEN MADE INTO A STURDY DINING TABLE. RUSTIC TWIG FURNISHINGS ARE USED THROUGHOUT THE ROOM. THE UNUSUAL CHANDELIER MIMICS A TEPEE.

OPPOSITE

THE OWNERS OF THIS WHITEFISH, MONTANA, RESIDENCE BY NORTHWOOD LOG HOMES CAN ENJOY PANORAMIC VIEWS FROM THEIR DINING ROOM. THE SEMICIRCULAR SHAPE OF THE DECK IS REPEATED IN THE WINDOWS AND TEPEE-STYLE CEILING. HIGHLY POLISHED LOGS FORM THE TABLE, WHILE CHAIRS, DRESSED IN THEIR ORIGINAL BARK, PLAY A SUPPORTING ROLE. THE BOLDLY PATTERNED NAVAJO RUG AND ANTLER CHANDELIER ADD VISUAL APPEAL.

ABOVE

THE DINING ROOM OF THIS RESIDENCE IN VAIL, COLORADO, BY ARCHITECT JIM MORTER SHOWS THE BEAUTIFUL WEDGEWOOD BLUE BUILT-IN CHINA CABINET, WHICH BRINGS THE FAMILY'S EXTENSIVE CHINA COLLECTION INTO THE DESIGN OF THE ROOM. THE COLOR IS A NICE CONTRAST TO THE RICH PATINA OF WOOD PANELING AND CEILING BEAMS.

BELOW

A PANOPLY OF SHAPES, TEXTURES, AND PERIODS IS FEATURED IN THE LIVING AND DINING AREAS OF THE SAME HOME, BUILT BY TIMBERPEG. ROCK, WOOD, AND FLAGSTONE ARE ENHANCED BY SKYLIGHTS. THE MISSION-STYLE DINING-ROOM FURNITURE CONTRASTS THE VICTORIAN GAME TABLE. A COLLECTION OF CLOCKS AND A GRACEFUL METALWORK CHANDELIER ARE OTHER POINTS OF INTEREST.

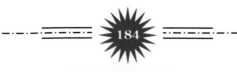

BELOW

ARCHITECT PHIL KORELL USED RED CEDAR TO CREATE HORIZONTAL AND VERTICAL LINES FOR THE DINING ROOM OF THE SNETETSE LODGE IN BITTEROOT VALLEY, MONTANA. THE INFLUENCE OF GUSTAV STICKLEY AND FRANK LLOYD WRIGHT IS SEEN IN THE DINING-ROOM TABLE, CHAIRS, AND GEOMETRIC CHANDELIER.

LEFT

LARGE CIRCULAR LOGS, WITH ALL OF NATURE'S IMPERFECTIONS IN ADDITION TO CARVED AND PAINTED EMBELLISHMENTS, ADD INTEREST TO THE VERTICAL AND HORIZONTAL LINES OF THE SNETETSE LODGE DINING ROOM. INTERIOR DESIGN IS BY KAREN KORELL; NEAL KORELL DESIGNED THE FURNTURE.

LEFT

THE ENGLISH ARTS & CRAFTS DINING CHAIRS, UPHOLSTERED IN A SOFT PEACH, GREEN, AND ECRU FRUIT-AND-FLORAL PRINT, BRING ANOTHER DESIGN PERIOD TO THIS WESTERN-STYLE ROOM. THE METALWORK CHANDELIER, AN EXACT COPY OF A MOLESWORTH DESIGN, FEATURES INDIANS CHASING BUFFALO, WHILE ON THE HIGHLY POLISHED TABLE WROUGHT-IRON CANDELABRAS CAST A WARM GLOW. AN ORIENTAL CARPET SOFTENS THE PLANK FLOORING.

ABOVE

ARCHITECT JOHN DOUGLAS LET THE STREAMLINED SHAPES IN THIS HOME SPEAK FOR THEMSELVES.
MINIMAL DECORATING AND DESIGN ENHANCE THE NEUTRAL, HIGHLY FUNCTIONAL SETTING, WHICH
MIXES WOOD, GLASS, AND CONCRETE BLOCK FOR A HOME THAT IS BEAUTIFUL IN ITS SIMPLICITY.
THE DINING CHAIRS SHOW A SLIGHT BIEDERMEIER INFLUENCE.

HIGH DRAMA IS EXPRESSED IN THE SHEER SIMPLICITY OF THIS DESIGN. CURVED STUCCO ARCHES ADD ARCHITECTURAL CONTRAST TO THE RECTANGULAR LINES OF THE DINING TABLE, THE RIVETING COLORS IN THE CONTEMPORARY PAINTING, AND THE MARBLE PEDIMENT THAT SERVES AS A PIECE OF ART. CURVED LINES ARE REPEATED IN THE ARMS OF THE CHAIRS AND LARGE POTTERY PIECES.

BELOW

THE STARK WHITE SIMPLICITY OF NANCY KITCHELL'S DESIGN IS SOFTENED BY THE ROUND PILLARS OF THE TABLE BASE, THE CONTOUR OF THE DINING CHAIRS AND THEIR SOFT GRAY-MAUVE UPHOLSTERY, AND THE SIMPLE POTTERY BOWL USED AS A CENTERPIECE. PLANTS ARE USED AS OTHER MINIMALIST DECORATIVE ELEMENTS.

ABOVE

ELEGANT DINING IS ACHIEVED IN THIS ALCOVE-STYLE ROOM CREATED BY DAVID MICHAEL MILLER ASSOCIATES. THE STUCCO ARCHWAY SUGGESTS INTIMATE DINING AROUND THE GLASS-TOPPED TABLE THAT RESTS ON A STONE BASE. THE HANDSOMELY CARVED CHAIRS ARE UPHOLSTERED IN OLD ORIENTAL CARPETING. THE TWO-TIERED WOODEN CHANDELIER HANGS FROM AN OVAL SOFFIT. CACTUS, FRAMED ART, AND A MAGNIFICENT FLORAL ARRANGEMENT ADD SOUTHWEST CHARM.

LEFT

THIS BRIGHT, SUNNY DINING ROOM OFFERS NOT ONLY FINE FARE FOR THE PALATE, BUT FOOD FOR THOUGHT FOR AVID COLLECTORS. VARIOUS PERIOD ANTIQUE FURNISHINGS ARE COMPLEMENTED BY THE UNUSUAL DINING CHAIRS, TAPESTRY WALL HANGING, AND BIRD CAGES CLEVERLY DISPLAYED THROUGHOUT THE ROOM. THE BRONZE CHANDELIER FEATURES A LEAF-AND-TASSLE PATTERN.

RIGHT

RED AND COBALT BLUE ARE THE COLORS CHOSEN TO ACCESSORIZE THIS HOME IN SANTA FE, NEW MEXICO. TRADITIONAL FURNISHINGS CONTRAST THE LOG *VIGAS* OF THE CEILING AND THE ADOBE KIVA-STYLE FIREPLACE. THE WROUGHT-IRON CHANDELIER AND MATCHING WALL SCONCE ARE GRACED BY EXQUISITE BLOWN-GLASS ORNAMENTS AND LIGHTS.

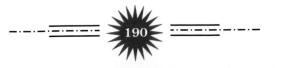

LEFT

THIS DINING ROOM EXPRESSES OLD WORLD ELEGANCE AND A BLEND OF RICH CULTURES. THE ORNATE CEILING IS REMINISCENT OF ITALIAN THEMES, WHILE THE FURNISHINGS REFLECT SPANISH AND MEXICAN INFLUENCES. THE ARCHES OF THE FIREPLACE AND PATIO WINDOW ARE MOORISH IN DESIGN. THE WROUGHT-IRON CHANDELIER AND WALL SCONCES ENHANCE THE EUROPEAN MOOD.

RIGHT

DESIGNER JULIA TOMETZ CREATED A QUIET, FORMAL MOOD FOR THIS DINING ROOM THAT MIXES SPANISH AND NATIVE AMERICAN INFLUENCES. THE CARVED-WOOD POSTS DEFINING THE ROOM'S ENTRY CREATE A THEME THAT'S REPEATED IN THE CARVED TABLE LEGS. THE WROUGHT-IRON CHANDELIER IS SPANISH IN DESIGN. THE WEAVINGS AND POTTERY ARE NATIVE AMERICAN.

BEDROOMS

SANCTUARIES FOR SOLACE

oday's *alcobas* have come a long way from the uncomfortable bedrolls that cowboys used to unfurl on hard ground. While that may seem a romantic tradition in Western novels, bedrooms today are often our favorite rooms for quiet repose and relaxation. They are intimate sanctuaries for solace that literally envelop us with the relics of our past, wrapping us in the warm blanket of history.

Bedrolls, futons, trundle beds, and bunks may be perfect for children's rooms, but adults like the comforting security of a real bed. Here, nestled against big patchwork pillows in a four-poster bed crafted of logs or an ornate Victorian made of burled walnut, one can bask in the memories of times past. Beds may be of brass or old white iron with paint that is slightly chipped. Twigs can be woven together

to create a restful haven. *Latillas* may form a headboard, or pillows can do the job. Sometimes a sleek contemporary theme is preferred, with a neutral color scheme for the walls, bedspread, and pillows.

Western-style bedrooms are the place for quilts and rag rugs, chintz and calico, pure white linens, and Hopalong Cassidy chenille bedspreads. Bedside tables piled with books, memorabilia, and flickering hurricane lamps are a must—although an artful chair can sometimes do double duty as a seat and table.

Samplers and shadowboxes made by great aunts and grandmothers are showcased in the bedroom as works of art. Family albums, frames filled with photographs of friends and ancestors, and trinkets from memorable occasions line bureau and dresser tops.

Old cupboards that stored clothes in an era when closets were either too

small or nonexistent now often hide televisions and stereo systems. Old trunks, some of which came West on covered wagons, now preserve out-of-season apparel or blankets.

Even when the bedroom is a loft in a new adobe dwelling, reached by a Pueblo-style ladder, there is a magical sense of seclusion in these latter-day hideaways where time stands still—if only for a moment of repose.

OPPOSITE: VICTORIAN SPLENDOR IS EVIDENT IN THIS FORMAL BEDROOM DESIGNED BY HASBROOK INTERIORS. THE BED WITH ITS REGAL CANOPY AND THE ORNATE CEILING TREATMENT ARE FOCAL POINTS. DELICATE PINK-AND-WHITE-SATIN STRIPES DRESS THE ROOM, WHILE THE ROCOCO GREEN NIGHTSTANDS AND TUFTED RED-VELVET CHEST ADD FRESH COLOR.

ABOVE

THE UPSTAIRS BEDROOM OF THIS HOME SHOWS A SPANISH MISSION
INFLUENCE WITH ITS ADOBE FIREPLACE AND HEAVY WOOD TREATMENT ON
DOORS LEADING INTO THE ROOM AND ONTO THE CHARMING
BALCONY. THE METAL BED IS SPANISH IN FEELING, WHILE THE
ARMOIRE IS ITALIANATE.

OPPOSITE

DESIGNER NANCY KITCHELL USED WHITE ACCESSORIES
THROUGHOUT THIS WHITE-BRICK BEDROOM TO SUGGEST A FEELING OF
SIMPLICITY AND SOLACE. SLEEP WOULD COME EASILY IN THIS SANCTUARY,
WITH ITS WHITE DUVET AND PILLOWS AND SIMPLE WHITE DRAPERIES.
THE CUSTOM-MADE IRONWORK BED HAS GRACEFUL CURVES
AND FILIGREE INSERTS.

BELOW

THIS BEDROOM MUST HAVE BEEN INSPIRED BY MOSQUITO
NETTING THAT IN OLDEN DAYS USED TO CLOISTER SUMMER BEDS. THIS
UPDATED VERSION BLENDS AN ELEGANT IRON BEDSTEAD WITH ORIENTAL
FURNISHINGS AND A MAGNIFICENT CARPET.

ABOVE

←──→

Work is merely an alcove away in the master bedroom of this residence
on Priest Lake, Idaho. A deck offers easy access to the splendid scenery. One could
also curl up with a good book from the family's library. The boldness of the logs is
softened by floral draperies, valances, and bedspread, as well as the patterns
of the Oriental rugs.

ABOVE

MONA SCOTT OF TIMBERCREEK DESIGNS IN CODY, WYOMING, CREATED THIS SETTING
FOR THE SWEETEST OF WESTERN DREAMS. THE LOG CABIN IS SOFTENED BY FLORAL UPHOLSTERY,
BED COVERINGS, AND PERIOD TAPESTRY. CURTAINS ARE DRAPED SIMPLY OVER LOG RODS SO
THAT THE VIEW IS NEVER BLOCKED. AN ANTIQUE CHEST AND A LOG-AND-ANTLER STEP
STOOL COMPLETE THE ROOM.

ABOVE

LEFT: THE BEDS IN THIS CHILD'S ROOM IN MONTANA ARE MADE OF UNPEELED LOGS.
A LOFT OVERLOOKS THE ROOM AND PROVIDES A GALLERY FOR PRIZED POSSESSIONS.
THE CARVED LAMP BASE REVEALS AN INDIAN IN A CANOE PUSHING DOWNSTREAM. *RIGHT:* THE
MASTER BEDROOM OF THE SAME RESIDENCE IS A BEAUTIFUL BLEND OF TEXTURES, COLOR, AND
NATURE. THE STONE FIREPLACE CONTRASTS THE DESIGN OF THE LOG BEAMS AND CEILING. THE
NIGHTSTANDS AND BEDSTEAD FEATURE PAINTED WOVEN *LATILLAS*.

OPPOSITE

WHAT YOUNGSTER WOULDN'T LOVE HANGING UP HIS DENIMS IN THIS BEDROOM? A SECOND
CHILD'S ROOM IN THE SAME HOME SPORTS TWIN BEDS OF WHITEWASHED PINE WITH WHITE QUILTED
DUVETS AND PILLOW-TICKING ACCESSORIES. A NAVAJO RUG, SNOWSHOES, A FEATHERED HEADDRESS,
AND A GENE AUTRY POSTER ALL SING THE WILD WEST'S PRAISES.

OPPOSITE

IN THE MASTER BEDROOM OF THIS HOME DESIGNED BY THE ARCHITECTURAL FIRM OF MORROW, BOWDEN, THE CEILING LOGS ACT AS A CANOPY, LEADING THE EYE TO THE PATIO AND POOL BEYOND. FURNISHINGS ARE SPARE, REFLECTING GUSTAV STICKLEY AND FRANK LLOYD WRIGHT INFLUENCES.

BELOW

WILD HORSES COULDN'T KEEP ONE FROM NAPPING IN THIS BEDROOM, DESIGNED BY CHRIS O'CONNELL. THE STONE FIREPLACE ADDS COLOR AND TEXTURAL INTEREST, AS DO THE OLD WOODEN TABLE AND CHESTS. THE COTTON "HORSEPLAY" BEDDING IS AN O'CONNELL DESIGN.

ABOVE

THIS IS A BEDROOM WHERE ONE CAN EASILY SAVOR QUIET MOMENTS. WINDOWS FLOOD THE ROOM WITH SUNLIGHT, AND THE WINDOWSEAT OFFERS A GREAT VIEW OF THE OUTDOORS. OLD-FASHIONED DESIGN ELEMENTS ABOUND: ORIENTAL CARPETS, PILLOWS AND DUST RUFFLES, FLORAL PILLOW SHAMS, QUILT TOPS, AND ART TREASURES. A FRENCH ARMOIRE CONTRASTS THE LOG PILLAR.

ABOVE

ONE COULD SNEAK AWAY TO THIS BEDROOM TO READ OR RELAX BY THE KIVA-STYLE
FIREPLACE. THE WHITE-STUCCO WALLS AND LOG CEILING ARE GIVEN TRADITIONAL TOUCHES
OF ELEGANCE IN THE ACANTHUS-LEAF FOUR-POSTER BED, THE CARVED CHEST, AND THE FLORAL-
PATTERN CARPET AND BEDSPREAD.

RIGHT

THIS RAMMED-EARTH HOME IN A TUCSON, ARIZONA, BARRIO WAS BUILT AND DESIGNED BY TOM WUELPERN. LOG BEAMS AND *LATILLAS* COVER THE CEILING, ADDING TEXTURAL INTEREST TO THE STUCCO WALLS. AN OLD IRON BED IS THE ROOM'S CENTERPIECE. AN ANGEL FRESCO KEEPS WATCH OVER FAMILY PORTRAITS IN UNUSUAL FRAMES. THE GREEN WOODWORK TRIM COMPLEMENTS THE ANGEL MURAL'S COLOR.

ABOVE

THIS BEDROOM AND ADJOINING SITTING ROOM WERE DESIGNED BY JULIA TOMETZ TO BE
A QUIET HAVEN OF REPOSE. WHITE-ADOBE WALLS ARE CONTRASTED WITH DARK WOOD *VIGAS*
AND *CORBELS* AND RICHLY CARVED HANDMADE CHESTS AND DOORS. A COLOR SCHEME OF BLACK,
GRAY, AND RED ACCENTS THE WHITE WALLS. NATIVE AMERICAN POTTERY, BASKETS,
AND WEAVINGS ADD APPEAL.

ABOVE

THE SOFT CREAM WALLS OF THIS BEDROOM ARE GIVEN DRAMATIC ACCENTS WITH THE HAND-CARVED BEDSTEAD, RICH TAPESTRY UPHOLSTERY AND PILLOWS, ORIENTAL CARPETS, AND THE PATINA OF THE ANTIQUE BLANKET CHEST. A FIREPLACE ADDS WARMTH AND COMFORT ON CHILLY EVENINGS. EVEN THE FAMILY DOG LIKES CURLING UP BY THE FIRE IN THIS BEDROOM.

ABOVE

THE MASTER BEDROOM OF THIS RESIDENCE IN RANCHO MIRAGE, CALIFORNIA, BLENDS
ORIENTAL AND CALIFORNIA DESIGN THEMES IN A MOOD OF QUIET ELEGANCE. FURNISHINGS, ART,
AND ACCESSORIES ALL SUGGEST ASIAN INFLUENCES. THE NEUTRAL WALLS AND CARPETING ARE A
FAVORITE CALIFORNIA THEME.

ABOVE

WHO WOULDN'T LOVE GREETING THE MORNING WHEN THE VIEW OFFERS A WESTERN
WAKE-UP CALL? DESIGNER NANCY KITCHELL LET NATURE TAKE THE LEAD IN THIS ROOM, WHICH
FEATURES MINIMAL OFF-WHITE CONTEMPORARY FURNISHINGS AND SELECT PIECES OF ART
AS ACCESSORIES.

ABOVE

THIS RESIDENCE IN RANCHO MIRAGE, A CLASSIC CALIFORNIA-STYLE REMODELING EFFORT BY THE
INSIGHT DESIGN TEAM, INCORPORATES A TASTEFULLY FURNISHED OFFICE IN THE MASTER BEDROOM.
FLOOR-TO-CEILING STORAGE AREAS PROVIDE A FUNCTIONAL DIVIDER.

OPPOSITE

THE INFLUENCE OF THE ORIENT ON CALIFORNIA DESIGN IS SEEN IN THE BEDROOM OF ANOTHER
RANCHO MIRAGE HOME. A WINDOW THAT HAD OFFERED A LACKLUSTER VIEW WAS REPLACED BY A
CLOSET WITH SHOJI SCREENS ADORNED WITH WOOD STRIPS.

FAMILY ROOMS

TROPHY ROOMS OF INTERIOR DESIGN

hink of Western-style family rooms as big, expansive areas perfect for casual entertaining, watching a large-screen TV, or even working on a home computer. Whether they're called dens or rumpus rooms or, as in Santa Fe, *lugares de retiro,* these multipurpose spaces are where family members can snuggle up by a fire, wrap themselves in a warm mohair throw, and read the latest Western novel or watch reruns of *Lonesome Dove.*

A fireplace is absolutely essential to the personality of the family room, which in newer homes is often built facing the patio. Since the family room is frequently used for informal entertaining, the proximity of the patio encourages an easy transition from the inside to the great outdoors. And since this is a room for reading as well as other leisurely pursuits, bookshelves usually line the walls, revealing the literary tastes of the family.

Television has become the all-seeing eye in every family room and is used not only for viewing but for playing computer games. It's also not uncommon to find a billiard table and bar in the family room—sometimes gen-

ABOVE: NICHOS DISPLAY SOUTHWESTERN TREASURES AND ARTIFACTS. *OPPOSITE:* READING IS A PLEASURE IN THIS SPANISH COLONIAL-STYLE LIBRARY.

uine antiques salvaged from an old ghost town or Western saloon.

Ceilings often feature *vigas* with hand-painted designs. Walls frequently have the added interest of *nichos,* where pottery and other artifacts are showcased. Tapestries and rugs not only grace tile or wooden floors, but hang decoratively on pine poles from the ceiling. Furnishings are plentiful and comfortable. Chairs, ottomans, and sofas are roomy and inviting; they may be upholstered in colorful patterns or in soothing neutrals. Tables are laden with books and papers, small lamps, and curio collections.

Western-style family rooms are museums of a sort—the perfect trophy rooms for displaying prized collections of Americana. Whether one collects beaded cradle boards or silver jewelry, Western art or old license plates, silver-embossed saddles and spurs, cowboy boots or Indian moccasins, the family room is an appropriate gallery for displaying valued treasures.

ABOVE

SIMPLE SHELVES BECOME PRESENTATION STAGES FOR THIS DRAMATIC COLLECTION OF BASKETS
AND POTTERY IN A FAMILY ROOM THAT IS SMALL ON SPACE BUT BIG ON CHARM.

OPPOSITE

THIS CONTEMPORARY FAMILY ROOM HAS A DISTINCTIVELY WESTERN FEELING, WITH ITS USE OF
BUILT-IN SHELVES DISPLAYING PRE-COLOMBIAN AND AZTEC COLLECTIONS. ANTIQUE HAND-CARVED
FURNISHINGS BALANCE THE COOL, MOUNTAIN-INSPIRED SHADES OF THE UPHOLSTERY.

OPPOSITE

THIS FAMILY-ROOM NOOK IS A BIBLIOPHILE'S PARADISE. WITH A COMFORTABLE CHAIR AND OTTOMAN POSITIONED JUST SO, THE SETTING IS IDEAL FOR A PERSON WHOSE LIFE REVOLVES AROUND READING AND COLLECTING BOOKS. EVEN THE CHAIRSIDE TABLE IS A HUMOROUS INTERPRETATION OF OVERSIZE BOOKS.

ABOVE

ECLECTIC DECORATING MAKES THIS DEN A PERFECT PLACE FOR ENTERTAINING. WOODEN CEILING BEAMS, A ROCK FIREPLACE, AND A NATIVE AMERICAN RUG ARE ACCENTED BY COMFORTABLE FURNISHINGS AND VARIOUS COLLECTIBLES, FROM POTTERY AND BASKETS TO EARLY-DAY WESTERN ART. THE ROOM IS OFF A SUNNY PATIO.

RIGHT

WHAT MORE DOES ONE NEED TO ENJOY LIVING IN THE WEST THAN A GREAT WINDOW THAT SHARES SUNLIGHT AND SCENERY? THIS ROOM, WITH ITS KNOTTY-PINE-PANELED WALLS AND BUILT-IN SOFA FLANKED WITH SOFT PILLOWS, IS A PERFECT PLACE FOR CONVERSATION—OR EVEN AN AFTERNOON NAP. AN OLD-FASHIONED ROLL-TOP DESK AND A LIBRARY CHAIR FACE THE SOFA.

INTERIOR DESIGN

LEFT

MOTHER NATURE JUST WALKS RIGHT IN AND MAKES HERSELF AT HOME IN THE GREAT ROOM OF THIS RESIDENCE IN MONTANA. COMFORTABLE CHAIRS PLACED AROUND AN UNUSUAL DRUM COFFEE TABLE AFFORD A PANORAMIC VIEW. ARCHITECT JERRY LOCATI USED LOGS AND LATTICEWORK WOOD TO CREATE A CORNICE EFFECT AT THE WINDOW.

OPPOSITE

THIS LOG-CABIN GREAT ROOM HAS COME A LONG WAY FROM ITS PREDECESSORS. ALTHOUGH THE SPACE IS SMALL, THE DESIGN IMPACT OF THE COZY ARRANGEMENT OF LEATHER AND UPHOLSTERY IS IMPRESSIVE. ART, SCULPTURE, AND RUGS ADD INTEREST, AS DOES THE OLD HORIZONTAL DRAWER CHEST THAT HAS ACQUIRED A NEW LIFE AS A COFFEE TABLE. THE HORIZONTAL THEME CONTINUES IN THE UNUSUAL WALL TREATMENT.

LEFT

A FAMILY READING ROOM IN THE WEST
IS NOT COMPLETE WITHOUT A FIREPLACE TO
PULL A CHAIR UP TO AND SETTLE IN FOR
AN ENGROSSING READ. THE CEILING-HIGH
STUCCO FIREPLACE IN THIS SUN VALLEY,
IDAHO, RESIDENCE IS ACCENTED BY
THE MANTEL IN A CONTRASTING COLOR.
CEILING BEAMS ADD RUSTIC INTEREST.
THE DESIGN IS BY NEIL WRIGHT.

BELOW

A SPANISH COLONIAL DESIGN THEME IS USED IN THIS FAMILY ROOM, AN IDEAL SPOT FOR INFORMAL ENTERTAINING, FRIENDLY CONVERSATION, AND GATHERING AROUND THE PIANO NESTLED AGAINST AN ADOBE WALL. A COMBINATION OF GRACEFUL CURVES, ARCHITECTURAL DRAMA, AND ANTIQUE FURNISHINGS DIGNIFIES THE ROOM, WHICH GIVES ONTO A SUN-DRENCHED PATIO.

ABOVE

THE LOOK AND FEEL OF AN EARLY-DAY LODGE WAS CREATED IN THIS MULTIPURPOSE ROOM FEATURING A VARIETY OF WESTERN DESIGN ELEMENTS. AMONG THEM ARE EXPOSED CEILING BEAMS, A WAGONWHEEL CHANDELIER, A ROCK FIREPLACE, *SALTILLO* TILE, HAND-CARVED FURNISHINGS, WROUGHT-IRON OCCASIONAL TABLES, AND LONGHORNS MOUNTED ABOVE THE DOOR. ART REPRESENTS EARLY WESTERN PERIODS, WHILE RUGS BLEND NAVAJO AND COWBOY THEMES.

BOOKS AND ANTLERS COZY UP TO EACH OTHER AT THE MOON CREST RANCH IN CODY, WYOMING. MONA SCOTT OF TIMBERCREEK DESIGNS HAD A FIELD DAY WITH ANTLERS, USING THEM IN LAMPS, COFFEE AND END TABLES, AND THE STRIKING CHANDELIER. A NAVAJO RUG PROVIDES A CONTRAST TO THE SPORTSMAN-THEME UPHOLSTERY OF THE WINGBACK CHAIR.

ABOVE

THE INTERPLAY OF DESERT COLORS AND GEOMETRIC NAVAJO PATTERNS IS AN EYE OPENER IN THIS
WESTERN FAMILY ROOM. SOFT YELLOW WALLS CONTRAST THE ASH-COLORED CABINETRY, WHICH
SHOWS OFF BASKETS, POTTERY, PRIMITIVE MASKS, AND SCULPTURE. TILE COUNTERTOPS FLANK
THE FIREPLACE. THE PRIMITIVE THEME IS REPEATED IN THE DRAWINGS ABOVE THE FIREPLACE
AND THE LARGE STONE PIECE SERVING AS A COFFEE-TABLE BASE.

ABOVE

BOOKSHELVES BECOME A CONTEMPORARY WORK OF ART IN THIS CRAFTSMAN-STYLE RESIDENCE
IN VENICE, CALIFORNIA. DISTINCTIVE SPACES FOR DISPLAYING SMALL ARTIFACTS AND COLLECTIBLES
HAVE BEEN CREATED BY MAKING SIX DIVISIONS IN THE BOOKCASE, WITH ANGULAR LINES LEADING
THE EYE TO THE CEILING DESIGN. GRAY-UPHOLSTERED FURNISHINGS ARE A NEUTRAL BACKDROP
FOR THE WOVEN NATIVE AMERICAN PILLOWS.

ABOVE

THE ARCHITECTURAL FIRM OF ROTH/SHEPPARD, WHICH BUILT THIS CABIN IN EVERGREEN,
COLORADO, CREATED A FAMILY ROOM MARKED BY RICH PANELING, WINDOWS TO TAKE IN
THE VIEW, AND A STRAIGHTFORWARD INTERIOR DESIGN THAT OFFERS MAXIMUM
FUNCTION FOR EASY ENTERTAINING.

PORCHES, PATIOS, GARDENS, AND POOLS

A STROLL DOWN NATURE'S PATH

What the pristine white veranda was to the East, the *portal* and the patio have become to the West. These are the places to bask in the sun and watch nature present an ever-changing show.

Formal *portales* often surround courtyards that are showpieces of outdoor ingenuity. Squared-off tree trunks become a floor or pathway, as do bricks, rocks, and flagstone. Built-in benches provide a theater for watching nature. Hollowed-out logs, stumps, and discarded troughs become window boxes. Redwood, twig, wicker, and rattan furnishings suggest easy informality. Terra cotta pots hold succulents and cacti. Wildflowers and ground cover, kissed by the sun and fanned by the wind, thrive in the gardens and on the patios of the West.

With trees overhead for a canopy, these patio and garden settings offer an opportunity for design that blends formal gardens with natural spaces—thus creating a juxtaposition that often blends the outside with the interior design of the home. These are settings that beg us to sit a spell and enjoy the fruits of nature. Western-style gardens are decidedly informal and casual. Nature is the queen here, and unlike those early settlers who had to spend so much of their energy fighting the elements, Western homeowners of today see their gardens as harmonizing rather than doing battle with natural forces. Gardens can now complement, rather than manipulate, their surroundings.

Twig and lodgepole-pine furnishings, along with wicker, are in their element here. So are old wheelbarrows, whiskey barrels, and ox carts that serve as pots for growing plants, flowers, and ornamental trees. Whimsical folk art adds another kind of color, texture, and interest. Stones and cacti become nature's sculptures.

Swimming pools have become a standard feature of Western homes. Their azure blue is a sparkling counterpoint to the patchwork greens and browns of the land. Their shapes are diverse—oval, rectangle, circle, and kidney—and most are accented with tile borders. Some even have artistic scenes painted on the bottom. All across the West, pools are a symbol of the carefree lifestyle, as well as a setting for casual lounging and entertaining.

OPPOSITE: AL FRESCO DINING CAN ALMOST BE A YEAR-ROUND TREAT AT THIS RESIDENCE IN COLUMBUS FALLS, MONTANA, BY ALPINE LOG HOMES AND LACHANCE BUILDERS. ARCHITECT JEFFERY BALCH DESIGNED THE HOME.

ABOVE

THIS POOL IN BOZEMAN, MONTANA, EASILY CONJURES UP IMAGES OF LAZY SUMMER DAYS.
THE HOME WAS DESIGNED BY MCLAUGHLIN ARCHITECTS.

OPPOSITE

TOP LEFT: THIS VIEW OF THE SAME BOZEMAN HOME SHOWS HOW THE ARCHITECT ECHOED THE
SHAPE OF SURROUNDING HILLS IN THE HOME'S CURVING WOODEN ARCHWAYS AND STONE RETAINING
WALLS. *BOTTOM LEFT:* A LARGE PICTURE WINDOW OFFERS YET ANOTHER VIEW OF THE MOUNTAIN
SETTING OF THE RESIDENCE. *TOP RIGHT:* THIS VIGNETTE OF THE DECK SHOWS HOW RED-CEDAR
BOARDS MAGNIFY THE HOME'S LINES. *BOTTOM RIGHT:* THE RESIDENCE'S IMPRESSIVE STONE-AND-
CEDAR ENTRYWAY HINTS AT THE BEAUTY TO BE FOUND INSIDE.

LEFT

THIS PATIO BECOMES AN EXTENSION OF THE HOME AND OFFERS A WEALTH OF WESTERN DESIGN IDEAS. THE CURVED COUNTERTOP TELLS A STORY IN TILE, WITH SMALL LEADED-GLASS WINDOWS SET IN FOR A PEEK AT THE SURROUNDING SCENERY. THE COUNTERTOP IS A SHOWCASE FOR PRIMITIVE POTTERY.

BELOW

AN EXTENDED VIEW OF THIS PATIO SHOWS HOW WELL THE POOL WORKS FOR YEAR-ROUND ENTERTAINING. POTTED PLANTS, RUSTIC FURNISHINGS, AND HUMOROUS SCULPTURES, INCLUDING A FAUX CROCODILE NOW USED AS A FLOWER PLANTER, ARE INTERESTING ELEMENTS. NOTE THE TABLE SET WITH CACTUS-DESIGN PLATES AND THE CACTUS CENTERPIECE.

OPPOSITE

DINING *AL FRESCO* IN THE WEST MEANS NATURE IS THE FIRST GUEST YOU INVITE TO SHARE YOUR REPAST. BLUE SKIES AND PLENTY OF TREES EMBRACE THIS FLAGSTONE PATIO WITH ITS ADOBE HORNO OVEN. TWIG FURNISHINGS, OLD SERAPES DRAPED OVER CHAIRS, AND AN ABUNDANCE OF FLOWERS MAKE THIS PATIO IN KETCHUM, IDAHO, PERFECT FOR CASUAL DINING.

ABOVE

THIS COVERED PORCH ON A LOG-AND-MORTAR CABIN IN KETCHUM, IDAHO, IS A GREAT PLACE
FOR GROWING PLANTS AND WATCHING NATURE AT WORK—AND IT'S A WONDERFUL SHOWCASE
FOR OLD-FASHIONED WESTERN ARTIFACTS. A SOFA IS COVERED WITH A NAVAJO BLANKET.
OLD FISHING GEAR, BOTH DECORATIVE AND FUNCTIONAL, IS ALWAYS READY FOR THE NEXT CATCH.

OPPOSITE

MONTANA LOG HOMES BUILT THIS RESIDENCE TO TAKE ADVANTAGE OF A MAGNIFICENT VIEW OF
FLATHEAD LAKE, MONTANA. THE LOG HOME BLENDS THE BEST OF OLD-FASHIONED RUSTIC
DESIGN—NOTCHED LOGS AND A TIN ROOF—WITH THE LATEST TECHNOLOGY. THE DECK WRAPS
AROUND THE HOUSE, GIVING THE FAMILY SUPERB VIEWS OF THE LAKE AND MOUNTAINS.

LEFT

SUN DRENCHES THE EXPANSIVE FRONT DECK OF THIS RESIDENCE IN SUN VALLEY, IDAHO. ARCHITECT NEIL WRIGHT DESIGNED THE HOME TO HAVE A LODGE FEELING, WITH ITS HEAVY STONE WALLS AND WALKWAYS, SHINGLED ROOF, ADOBE EXTERIOR, AND HEAVY TIMBERED BEAMS.

BELOW

THE ENTRYWAY OF THE SAME RESIDENCE IS WESTERN AT ITS BEST. THE FLAGSTONE PATIO BLENDS WELL WITH THE STACKED-STONE WALLS AND HEAVY TIMBERED EAVES THAT PROVIDE SHADE. RUSTIC WOODEN BENCHES INVITE REPOSE. THE SPANISH COLONIAL WROUGHT-IRON LAMPS CAST A WELCOME GLOW FOR EVENING ENTERTAINING.

OPPOSITE

FOR A QUIET PLACE TO COMMUNE WITH NATURE, THIS TINY PATIO IS PERFECT. HAND-CARVED FURNISHINGS SEEM RIGHT AT HOME, SURROUNDED BY BRUSH AND ASPEN AND MAJESTIC NEARBY MOUNTAINS.

ABOVE

⬅———————————————————————————➡

ARCHITECT JAMES D. MORTON CREATED A BEAUTIFUL BLEND OF RUSTIC AND CONTEMPORARY
DESIGN FOR THIS FAMILY'S BIG SKY, MONTANA, HOME.

OPPOSITE

⬅———————————————————————————➡

THIS BEAUTIFUL GARDEN IN OJAI, CALIFORNIA, NOT ONLY PRESENTS A BLAZE OF BRILLIANT COLORS,
BUT ALSO OFFERS A VISTA THAT STRETCHES THE EYE.

LEFT

ARCHITECT JACKIE MOWRY USED A TRADITIONAL ADOBE *HACIENDA* DESIGN IN HER HOME, WHICH FEATURES A COVERED PATIO. WEATHERED LOG BEAMS AND *CORBELS* ADD RUSTIC CHARM. A BRICK WALKWAY EXTENDS FROM THE PATIO AND MAKES A GREAT SETTING FOR *AL FRESCO* ENTERTAINING. THE LUSH LAWN AND OLD CEDAR TREES COMPLEMENT THE SETTING.

OPPOSITE

SPANISH AND MEXICAN THEMES ARE EVIDENT IN THIS SMALL BRICK PATIO THAT LETS NATURE PROVIDE MOST OF THE SHADE. PAINTED FURNITURE, IN THE TRADITIONAL MEXICAN BLUE, AND COLORFUL UPHOLSTERY AND TABLE COVERINGS MAKE THIS SECLUDED SPOT A HAVEN FOR RELAXATION AND ENTERTAINING.

FURNISHINGS WITH A WESTERN SPIRIT

Walk into any home that is decorated Western style and you don't have to wonder about the interests of the owners. Icons of the West will abound—buffalo silhouettes, Indian symbols, cowboy trappings, and the like. There's a definite spirit—the French would call it *élan*—about furnishings with a Western flair.

You also don't have to wonder about the owners' values: Cowboy and Neo-Cowboy styles (including furnishings and accessories from the 1930s and '40s) glorify old-fashioned beliefs that existed when the West was a land of wide-open spaces and pioneers strove to create a new life. Both styles convey a warmth, a sense of romance and adventure, and above all an easy, functional informality that is the essence of the West.

There are no rules about furnishing in the Western spirit, so breathe a sigh of relief. The finished design is limited only by one's imagination—and one's diligence in seeking relics of the West and then arranging them in fresh, new ways.

Western-style furnishings blend Rustic and Ranch, function and art, Southwest and the latest Neo-Cowboy fashion. It easily mixes new with old.

It's also not uncommon to find a vintage piece of Victorian or Chinese Chippendale residing happily beside a Rustic leather couch or standing near a sturdy harvest table.

Ancestral portraits framed in silver look quite appropriate hanging beside a Georgia O'Keeffe watercolor or a William Acheff oil painting. Old farm and ranch tools are assigned places of honor above the mantel, just like hunting trophies. A fine porcelain vase may become the perfect accompaniment to a pair of silver spurs. Molesworth, Stickley, and Biedermeier chairs easily sit side by side—as different in design and style as their makers were in character, yet wonderfully compatible.

Western is the only melting-pot style of decorating that fosters such a comfortable marriage of period and tradition, artifact and memorabilia. A period hutch that once housed bone china may now be the perfect showcase for a cowboy-boot collection. A crystal chandelier may have been relegated to the

OPPOSITE: DESIGNER SUSAN WUNDERLICH OF CHICAGO COVERED THIS MAGNIFICENT CLUB CHAIR FROM THE 1920S WITH A BEACON BLANKET WOVEN TWO DECADES LATER.

ABOVE: ANTLER CHANDELIERS SHED THEIR SPECIAL LIGHT ALL ACROSS THE WEST, REFLECTING AN INNOVATIVE WAY OF RECYCLING NATURE'S CAST-OFFS. THIS PIECE, MADE BY ARTE DE MEXICO, HAS BASES FOR SMALL MICA LAMPSHADES THAT CAST A SOFT, LOVELY GLOW.

attic, replaced by a chandelier made of antlers—or metalwork depicting a rodeo scene. A traditional four-poster mahogany bed may be traded for one made of barnwood, lodgepole pine, or burled roots. An English-style coffee table may be shoved aside in favor of an old-fashioned painted sleigh. Ordinary shelving for knickknacks may be relegated to the basement, replaced by the top part of a rowboat or canoe. Even a swimming pool's diving board may be tossed aside in favor of an old buckboard wagon.

Central to this design style is the definition of the word *landscape.* In Western design, a room itself is viewed as a landscape, with colors, textures, and heights adding the same elements of interest that they would out of doors.

Western design also encourages a rich blend of nostalgia—not the nostalgia of the prim Victorian period, but a desire to preserve the trappings of the most colorful region of the country.

Says J. Mike Patrick, whose Cody, Wyoming, company, New West, grew out of an interest in reproducing Thomas Molesworth designs: "No part of the United States has ever captured the hearts and minds of the American people as has the West. . . . (It) has meant opportunity and freedom. Western design reflects that character. It tends to be casual, warm, friendly, utilitarian and makes wonderful use of the materials and native traditions of the West. Above all, Western design is quintessentially American."

ABOVE: THE MAGNIFICENT PAIR OF CARVED PHEASANTS ON THIS BIEDERMEIER SOFA SYMBOLIZE THE CLASSICAL STYLE THAT SWEPT THE WORLD AFTER 1790. IT BEGAN TO APPEAR IN FURNITURE OF THE WESTERN FRONTIER SOME 50 TO 60 YEARS LATER. *OPPOSITE:* A TRADITIONAL NEW MEXICAN *VIGA* CEILING AND WROUGHT-IRON CHANDELIER CREATE A COZY DINING ATMOSPHERE. THE COUNTRY-STYLE PINE TABLE AND CHAIRS FORM A STYLISTIC COUNTERPOINT TO THE ELEGANT EUROPEAN ARMOIRE.

DECORATING THE COWBOY WAY

Without doubt, the single most important catalyst for Western-style interior decor was Thomas Canada Molesworth. From the 1930s through the '50s, he was considered the leading light of Western design, and deservedly so.

After service in World War I, Molesworth's exposure to furniture making and design began when he was employed by Rowe Furniture in Billings, Montana. Visits to the Chicago Furniture Mart honed his creative abilities. In 1931, Molesworth moved his family to Cody, Wyoming, where he established the Shoshone Furniture Company.

Molesworth's work surpassed that of early-day cowboys, who lacked fine wood and precise tools; indeed, in those days, function mattered far more

ABOVE: THOMAS MOLESWORTH'S DESIGN TALENT COULD EMBRACE BOTH THE RUSTIC AND THE URBANE. THIS UPHOLSTERED ARMCHAIR OFFERS A WESTERN REFERENCE IN THE PINE-BRANCH DESIGN, BUT WITH A JAPANESE SENSE OF FORMALISM. THE STRUCTURE AND STYLE OF THE CHAIR CAPTURE THE STREAMLINED TAILFIN MANIA OF THE POST-WORLD WAR II PERIOD.

than style. In contrast, Molesworth created sturdy yet finely crafted furniture and accessories that appealed as much to Western cowboys as they did to rich Easterners imbued with the rugged romance of the West. He was known for unique furniture fashioned of antlers, lodgepole pine, and hand-peeled fir dressed in rawhide, Indian blankets, and animal skins. Steer horns and shiny nail heads were typical Molesworth embellishments.

Many of Molesworth's pieces were adorned with elaborate dioramas designed by his associate Thomas Grigware—he graced cupboards with scenes from nature and silhouetted animals against light shades and fire-screens. The most popular motif was a bowlegged cowboy silhouette, a design theme evident in many furnishings now patterned in the Molesworth tradition.

ABOVE: FROM 1931 TO 1977, THOMAS MOLESWORTH CREATED AN UTTERLY UNIQUE COLLECTION OF WESTERN FURNITURE KNOWN AS MOLESWORTH STYLE, COWBOY HIGH STYLE, OR NORTHERN ROCKIES STYLE. THOUGH BEST KNOWN FOR HIS BIG, BURLY COUCHES, MOLESWORTH DEMONSTRATED A MORE REFINED AND CLASSICAL PROFILE IN THIS HANDSOME CHAIR-AND-SETTEE GROUPING ADORNED WITH CARVED NATIVE AMERICAN SWASTIKA SYMBOLS.

BELOW

AN INTIMATE KITCHEN OR BREAKFAST TABLE BY THOMAS MOLESWORTH IS ANCHORED IN THE CENTER BY A LARGE BURL. THE TABLE AND MATCHING CHAIRS WITH FABRIC CUSHIONS REPRESENT THE RUSTIC AND NATURAL ASPECT OF MOLESWORTH'S FURNISHINGS.

ABOVE

THIS UNIQUE CABINET WAS DESIGNED TO HOLD A COMPLETE SILVER SERVICE. THOMAS MOLESWORTH INTEGRATED MATERIALS IN THE RUSTIC STYLE—WORM-EATEN WOOD— WITH THE UNUSUAL FUNCTIONAL DEMANDS OF THE CABINET TO PRODUCE A SUBLIME COMPOSITION. THE FURNITURE'S MOST IMPRESSIVE QUALITY IS ITS IMPECCABLE ATTENTION TO PROPORTION AND SCALE.

ABOVE

A CARVED HORSEHEAD IS THE DRAMATIC CENTERPIECE OF A TWIN-SIZE BEDSTEAD BY THOMAS MOLESWORTH. THE CARVING WAS PRODUCED BY A LOCAL WYOMING CRAFTSMAN AND FRAMED BY DISTINCTIVE MOLESWORTH STYLING.

BELOW

THE RUSTIC AND THE REFINED ARE MARRIED IN THIS FINE BED BY THOMAS MOLESWORTH. THE FURNITURE PIECE IS A STUDY IN JUXTAPOSITIONS: A PLAIN HEADBOARD CONTRASTS THE ELABORATE FOOTBOARD, WHILE VERTICAL POSTS ARE OFFSET BY THE HORIZONTAL RHYTHM CREATED BY THE TOP HEADBOARD RAILS.

FROM RUSTIC TO RANCH STYLE

Leather and oak, never plastic, are benchmarks of Western design, especially when the style is Ranch or Rustic.

Ranch-style furnishings tend to have a sturdier, stouter appearance, while Rustic is usually associated with the one-of-a-kind twig and root furnishings often made by craftsmen who found beauty in wood's idiosyncrasies. However, Rustic and Ranch styles are alike in their homespun simplicity. Nicks and scars, scratches and peeling paint, the twists and burls in roots and twigs—these imperfections are considered badges of honor.

The elements of early ranch life are completely at home in this category. They are transformed into prized treasures for interior design, but when the real thing can't be found, reproductions or new pieces inspired by rustic furnishings always suffice.

Old branding irons are now candlesticks. Cowboy boots are bookends and doorstops. Old whiskey or pickle barrels are cut down to hold everything from magazines to skis. Saddles or lariats line a stairway or hang from a loft railing. Tired cowboy hats hang on a kitchen or bedroom wall.

Comfortable is the key word here—easy living is the hallmark of Ranch- or Rustic-style decorating.

ABOVE: COVERT WORKSHOPS OF CODY, WYOMING, FUSES A RUSTIC "PILLOW BENCH" WITH LEATHER AND BEADWORK PILLOWS BY QUEEN OF THE PLAINS.

ABOVE: HORNS SERVED NUMEROUS PURPOSES—AS BASES FOR CHAIRS AND TABLES AND AS HAT AND CLOTHES HOOKS. IN THIS HAT RACK, HORNS ARE ATTACHED TO AN OAK PLAQUE. *BELOW:* THESE BOOTS WEREN'T MADE FOR WALKING, BUT THEY SURE SERVE WELL AS A DOORSTOP IN A SANTA FE, NEW MEXICO, HOME. ONCE A COWBOY'S BEST FRIEND, ALONG WITH HIS HORSE AND SADDLE, BOOTS—REAL AND FAUX—NOW WALK A DUAL PATH AS DESIGN ACCESSORIES, GRACING MANTELS, HANGING ON WALLS, OR JUST LINED UP AT THE FOOT OF A BED FOR SHOW.

ABOVE: NATIVE AMERICAN ARTIFACTS, INCLUDING A TAOS DRUM, A PACIFIC NORTHWEST CHILDREN'S BENCH, AND BEADED POUCHES SURROUND A TOWERING ANTIQUE PAINTED WARDROBE.

ABOVE

ALTHOUGH THIS SIDE TABLE LOOKS AS IF IT CAME FROM THE ERA OF ADIRONDACK FURNISHINGS, IT IS A NEW CREATION, MADE BY DIANE COLE OF BOZEMAN, MONTANA. SHE USED MOSAIC TWIG WORK AND A NORTHERN PLAINS INDIAN DESIGN FOR THIS MODERN VERSION, COMPLETE WITH A TWIG FOR THE DRAWER PULL.

LEFT

THIS UNUSUAL WESTERN CABINET BY COVERT WORKSHOPS HAS VERSATILE STORAGE USES AND GENEROUS PANELS FOR CARVED WESTERN DECORATIONS. THE CABINET IS MADE OF PEELED AND SANDED FIR BRANCHES.

LEFT

Jimmy Covert's Cody, Wyoming, workshop is inspired by the legacy of Thomas Molesworth, but adds a naturalistic and frontier quality to its furniture. This letter desk is crafted of driftwood, cherry wood, and root burl. The bronze drawer pulls and cow skulls are by Peter Fillerup.

BELOW

Covert Workshops combines driftwood, cedar, walnut, ebony, root burl, bronze, and leather in the Keeksa Letter Desk. The central carved icon is a raven or "Keeksa"—a fitting symbol for a letter desk, since the blackbird is a messenger.

LEFT

Lamps that light up the West are made from just about everything: cowboy boots, old churns, even antlers. This one has an old branding iron for a base and stirrup appendages. The lamp shade is of rawhide, bound in leather strips and laces. A cord tassel serves as the light pull.

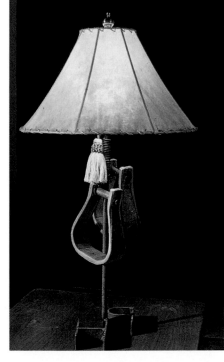

FROM FUNCTION TO ART FORM

When Thomas Molesworth and Gustav Stickley were creating functional chairs and other furnishings in the early 1900s, they probably had little idea that their work would someday be viewed as a valuable regional art form.

Stickley was a cabinet maker and superb craftsman who encouraged what he termed simple, straightforward, honest design. His furniture was called Craftsman or Mission style and was made of solid oak, trimmed with leather or wrought metal.

Like Molesworth's designs, Stickley's are now being reinterpreted for those who appreciate the Mission style. After a hiatus, Stickley's company is back in business and reissuing old plans, so people can build these furnishings for themselves.

The streamlined looks of Stickley chairs and tables seem inspired or at least influenced by Frank Lloyd Wright. Like Biedermeier pieces, they blend harmoniously with genuinely Western design.

ABOVE: A SUBLIME SIDEBOARD BY L. & J.G. STICKLEY, INC., EXPRESSES ITS CHARACTER THROUGH THE SIMPLE VARIATION OF THE CENTRAL-DRAWER WIDTHS AND SLIGHTLY CANTED OR ANGLED LEGS.

BELOW: L. & J.G. STICKLEY, INC., PRODUCED AN IMPOSING CASE CLOCK IN WHICH SIMPLE DETAILS ARE RENDERED IN PERFECT HARMONY.

ABOVE: OCCASIONALLY, CRAFTSMAN FURNITURE WAS EMBELLISHED WITH SIMPLE CARVINGS OR INLAID DESIGNS, AS CAN BE SEEN HERE IN THE CHAIR BACK AND TABLE LEGS. THIS ATTRACTIVE CORNER GROUPING ILLUSTRATES THE PERFECT USE OF THE CRAFTSMAN PICTURE MOLDING AND TRADEMARK HIGH PANELING.

ABOVE

LEFT: CRAFTSMAN-STYLE FURNITURE DESIGNERS DELIGHTED IN CIRCULAR AND OVAL SHAPES FOR TABLES. THIS BEAUTIFUL CUTOUT TABLE HAS A LOWER SHELF, A TYPICAL EXPRESSION OF THE CRAFTSMAN ETHIC OF UTILITY. *RIGHT:* BERKELEY MILLS FURNITURE HAS SOFTENED THE LINES OF ITS ARTS AND CRAFTS PIECES, GIVING THIS LEATHER-AND-HARDWOOD ARMCHAIR A CONTEMPORARY, ALMOST AERODYNAMIC APPEARANCE.

RIGHT

THE IRWIN HOUSE IN PASADENA, CALIFORNIA—A CRAFTSMAN MASTERPIECE BY GREENE AND GREENE—ILLUSTRATES A MORE REFINED AND INTEGRATED STYLE WHERE GRACEFUL CURVING LINES INTRODUCE A TOUCH OF ART NOUVEAU AND JAPANESE INFLUENCE.

CLASSIC CRAFTSMAN-STYLE FURNITURE, INCLUDING MORRIS ARMCHAIRS, A COPPER TABLE LAMP, A SETTLE, AND A BOOKCASE, PERFECTLY COMPLEMENT A DEN BUILT IN CONTEMPORARY CRAFTSMAN STYLE.

BELOW

WILLIAM GRUEBY PERFECTED THE ART OF APPLYING MATTE GLAZES TO POTTERY MADE IN BOSTON FROM 1898 TO 1909. GRUEBY'S RICH GREEN GLAZE WAS A CRAFTSMAN-STYLE SENSATION.

LEFT

A DRAMATIC CROSS-BRACE IS JOINED TO THE TABLE LEGS BY EXPOSED AND PEGGED TENONS IN THIS DINING TABLE BY THE STICKLEY BROTHERS COMPANY.

ABOVE

THE CARVED, SCROLLED ARMS OF THIS UPHOLSTERED SOFA, IN THE FORM OF A WATER CREATURE, DENOTE THE NEOCLASSICAL INFLUENCE OF THE BIEDERMEIER STYLE, INTRODUCED TO THE WESTERN FRONTIER BY GERMAN IMMIGRANT FAMILIES AFTER 1840.

LEFT

AMERICAN FURNITURE BEFORE THE CIVIL WAR WAS HEAVILY INFLUENCED BY EUROPEAN CLASSICAL STYLES, INCLUDING BIEDERMEIER. ROUND TABLES LIKE THE ONE PICTURED HERE WERE OFTEN USED FOR CARD GAMES.

BELOW

THE LOVELY CURVED-BACK DESIGN OF THIS CHAIR, WITH AN IMPLIED VASE SHAPE IN THE CENTER, IS TYPICAL OF THE VIENNESE ELEGANCE THAT HEAVILY INFLUENCED GERMAN FURNITURE DESIGN DURING THE BIEDERMEIER PERIOD. SOME OF THIS FURNITURE WOULD APPEAR DECADES LATER IN PROSPEROUS HOMES OF THE AMERICAN WEST.

ABOVE

A STATELY BIEDERMEIER ARMOIRE OFFERS SIMPLIFIED CLASSICAL DETAILS SUCH AS FLANKING GILDED COLUMNS, A SUBTLE PEDIMENT AT THE TOP, AND AN ARCHITECTURAL DOOR-PANEL DESIGN.

THE NEO-COWBOY STYLE

Sometimes it's called "cowboy chic," sometimes "cowboy kitsch." One scribe dubbed it "Roy Rogers meets Michael Graves." Whatever it's called, however, the Neo-Cowboy style amounts to a stylistic reinterpretation that brings the designs of the West to devotees as far East as New York.

Like every other facet of Western design, the Neo-Cowboy style lassos its lineage from the past, using traditional materials—leather, rawhide, metal, and wood (especially oak, walnut, and mahogany). Neo-Cowboy is never made from sawdust and glue. No piece ever turns out quite like another. Like its ancestors, it is built to last and is based on the Western lifestyle.

Neo-Cowboy furnishings have a dash of Western humor. Gunslinger chairs, with their rendering of a gunfighter in wood on the back, are in vogue. So are beds painted with singing cowboys. But don't call these creations a spoof. They are all inspired by a respect for the cowboy lifestyle. And Neo-Cowboy usually fits its owners' lifestyle perfectly, whether they are real ranching folks or just cowboy wannabes.

Those who create furnishings for this new breed of Western aficionado see design from a different vantage point—a weathered wooden fence is not just a relic, but raw material for new furnishings. Regardless of the artisan making Neo-Cowboy furnishings and accessories, the unifying theme is the use of fine indigenous woods, accented with cutouts, leather, stone, and canvas.

LEFT: A CLASSIC CHAIR IN THE MOLESWORTH STYLE, MADE OF ANTLER AND BURLED FIR BY SWEETWATER RANCH, IS UPHOLSTERED WITH CHIMAYO TAPESTRY FROM NORTHERN NEW MEXICO.

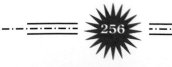

Below: Just a few blocks from downtown Cody, Wyoming, is situated this gem of a cabin furnished with Molesworth originals and lovingly preserved by its current owners. Easily recognizable are the burled-fir love seat upholstered in Chimayo weaving, the cutout-cowboy armchair, and the burled-fir floor lamp with a cowhide shade.

Above: Thomas Molesworth's famous "cutout cowboy" design motif was derived from a painting by Cody, Wyoming, artist Edward Grigware. Many contemporary "Molesworth Revival" furniture designers have elaborated on the cutout-cowboy and horse shapes, producing convincing illusions such as this horsehead-and-cowboy chest of drawers produced by Sweetwater Ranch of Cody.

BELOW

BURLED WOOD, CAUSED BY A DEFORMITY IN THE TREE, IS COMMONLY USED IN VENEERS AND INLAYS. DESIGNER THOMAS MOLESWORTH GOT THE NOTION TO USE THE ENTIRE BURL AS A STRUCTURAL RATHER THAN STRICTLY DECORATIVE ACCENT. IN SO DOING, HE INVENTED A NEW LOOK IN WESTERN DESIGN. SWEETWATER RANCH'S CONTEMPORARY BURLED ARMCHAIR IS UPHOLSTERED IN POPULAR PENDLETON FABRIC, A PERENNIAL WESTERN CLASSIC.

ABOVE

SWEETWATER RANCH COMBINES THE LUXURIOUS TEXTURES OF CHIMAYO WEAVING AND SMOOTH SUEDE IN THIS MOLESWORTH BURLED-FIR ARMCHAIR.

LEFT

THOMAS MOLESWORTH LIKED TO BUILD ROUNDED AND OCCASIONALLY OCTAGONAL TABLES. SWEETWATER RANCH CONTINUES THIS TRADITION, UTILIZING A SET OF FASCINATING BURLED LOGS FOR TABLE LEGS.

RIGHT

GIANT STRUCTURAL LOGS, RIVER-ROCK BOULDER MASONRY, AND EXPANSIVE WINDOWS ARE COMBINED BY ARCHITECT JERRY LOCATI IN A DRAMATIC TOUR DE FORCE IN THIS MONTANA HOME. THE UPSTAIRS FOYER IS FURNISHED WITH A PAIR OF MOLESWORTH-STYLE SOFAS. THE HOME WAS BUILT BY REICHSTETTER CONSTRUCTION.

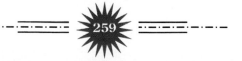

FURNISHINGS WITH A WESTERN SPIRIT

LEFT

THIS MOLESWORTH-STYLE SIDEBOARD FROM SWEETWATER RANCH IS CRAFTED OF SLENDER LODGEPOLES THAT CASCADE TO THE FLOOR AT THE CORNERS. NOTE THE RHYTHMIC, FORMAL PLACEMENT OF THE IRREGULARLY SHAPED ANTLER PULLS AGAINST THE WOOD—THE FEELING THEY CREATE IS ONE OF ZEN-LIKE DYNAMISM.

RIGHT

THOMAS MOLESWORTH LOVED TO DESIGN ENTIRE ROOMS IN HIS UNMISTAKABLE STYLE. IN HIS LIFETIME, HE COMPLETED NUMEROUS LARGE-SCALE DESIGN COMMISSIONS FOR DUDE RANCHES OF WEALTHY CORPORATE BARONS. THIS LIVING-ROOM SHOWCASE OF MOLESWORTH FURNITURE BY SWEETWATER RANCH ILLUSTRATES MANY OF THE DESIGNER'S FAVORITE EFFECTS, SUCH AS BURLED FURNITURE, CLASSIC WESTERN UPHOLSTERY, CUTOUT SILHOUETTE SHAPES, AND LODGEPOLE REFINEMENT.

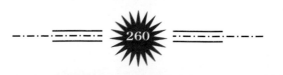

BELOW

HUTCHINSON, KANSAS, CRAFTSMAN MIKE LIVINGSTON EMBELLISHED HIS ARROWHEAD CHEST WITH HIS OWN CUSTOM-DESIGNED HARDWARE.

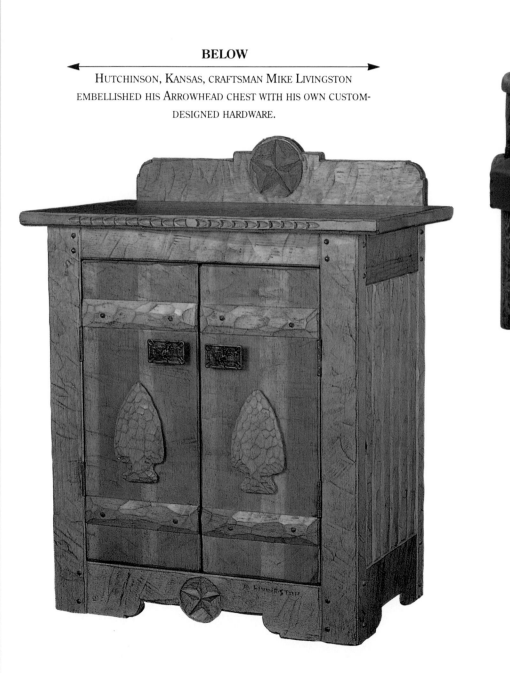

ABOVE

SWEETWATER RANCH'S LODGEPOLE-AND-BURL ARMCHAIR IS BOLDLY ASSERTIVE WITH ITS SCARLET UPHOLSTERY AND BRONZE PLAQUE WITH ROCKY MOUNTAIN RAMS.

THE SOUTHWEST STYLE

Long after Coronado and the Conquistadors left their mark on the Southwest, the vestiges of their lifestyle remain. Spanish missions inspired by pueblos and Baroque, Byzantine, and Renaissance architecture are graceful reminders of the West's history.

The design that complements Spanish-style homes draws its inspiration from ornate ethnic influences— Moorish, Medieval, Roman, and Renaissance. It is crossbreeding at its best. The Spanish colonials lived well and had a strong sense of beauty and style.

Missions played an important role in family, social, and economic life at this time. It is no surprise that so many features of the Spanish Colonial style show the pervasive influence of the Roman Catholic Church.

Primitive ornamental mission doors are official greeters. Interior

ABOVE: THIS CLASSIC NEW MEXICAN *TRASTERO,* OR CUPBOARD, BY GREG FLORES OF TAOS, HAS NATIVE AMERICAN AND SPANISH MOTIFS. *OPPOSITE:* THE SOUTHWESTERN-STYLE ENTRANCE HALL OF THIS SANTA FE HOUSE COMBINES ADOBE WITH HEAVY DOORS AND ORIENTAL HALL FURNITURE.

walls can be the white or cream of missions or the rich organic shades of terra cotta, raspberry, purple, brilliant gold, chocolate brown, orange, saffron, or pumpkin.

Furnishings are a tasteful montage of elegance and simplicity, traditional and Spanish Colonial, wicker and wood. Upholstery may be leather, woven blankets, or heavy fabrics in rich colors. Old ironwork becomes a base for glass-topped tables.

Trasteros and chests—simple or richly carved—and wooden benches and *bancos* are also standard features. So is heavy ironwork hardware. Colorful tiles outline fireplaces, stairways, and counter tops; *saltillo* tile is popular for flooring. Accessories include baskets and pottery, punched-tin mirror and picture frames, chile *ristras, santos*, lanterns, ironwork candleholders, and primitive folk art. Weavings can be used as upholstery, tablecloths, wall art, or rugs.

BELOW

THE NAVAJO CHIEF THRONE BY JEREMY MORRELLI OF SANTA FE, NEW MEXICO, IS A LIVELY MIXTURE OF PUEBLO DECO, CHIPPENDALE, AND TRADITIONAL NEW MEXICAN STYLES.

ABOVE

MASTER CRAFTSMAN JEREMY MORRELLI OF SANTA FE REPRODUCES A STUNNING SIDEBOARD INFLUENCED BY THE CARVING OF TAOS MASTER NICOLAI FECHIN. THE DOG AND BIRD DESIGNS ARE NATIVE AMERICAN IN ORIGIN.

BELOW

THIS HANDSOME LOUNGE-STYLE BENCH, A PERFECT ADDITION TO ANY SANTA FE-STYLE LIVING ROOM OR GREAT ROOM, IS COVERED WITH NATIVE AMERICAN-DESIGN FABRIC BY PENDLETON MILLS OF OREGON.

ABOVE

A MODEST SIDECHAIR BECOMES A
MASTERPIECE WHEN DESIGNED BY NICOLAI
FECHIN, WHO PRACTICED HIS UNIQUE BLEND
OF RUSSIAN FOLK ART AND NEW MEXICAN
FURNITURE IN TAOS FROM 1927 TO 1933.
THE CLASSIC DESIGN IS REPRODUCED BY
JEREMY MORRELLI OF SANTA FE.

LEFT

THIS BEAUTIFUL CABINET DESIGNED BY
ANNE GALE INCORPORATES PUNCHED-TIN
INSET PANELS AND A CARVED *DICHO*, OR
SAYING. THE APHORISM—"DIOS TARDA PERO
NO OLVIDA"—DECLARES THAT GOD DELAYS,
BUT DOES NOT FORGET.

BELOW

MIKE LIVINGSTON OF HUTCHINSON, KANSAS, IS A MASTER CARVER WITH A ROMANTIC STYLE INCORPORATING ICONOGRAPHY OF THE OLD WEST AND THE SOUTHWEST. THIS CHEST PAYS HOMAGE TO NEW MEXICAN FURNITURE AND SPANISH COLONIAL RELIGIOUS SYMBOLS.

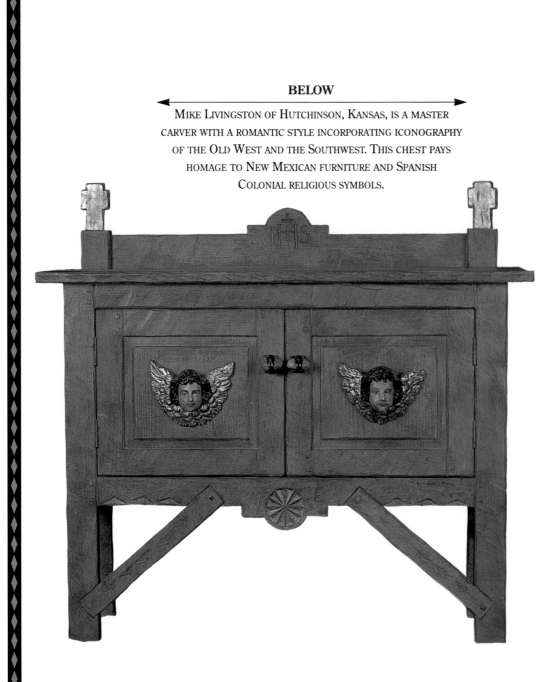

ABOVE

THIS NEW MEXICAN SIDE CHAIR BY CHRIS SANDOVAL OF ALBUQUERQUE OFFERS A STREAMLINED STYLING MADE POPULAR DURING THE SPANISH COLONIAL REVIVAL OF NEW MEXICO IN THE 1930S. THE LEATHER STRAP-WORK CHAIR IS SHOWN IN FRONT OF A KIVA-STYLE FIREPLACE.

OPPOSITE

A SOUTHWESTERN LIVING ROOM BOASTS A VARIETY OF WESTERN ARTIFACTS, INCLUDING A COWBOY BOOT-'N'-SADDLE LAMP AND A PACIFIC NORTHWEST TOTEM SCULPTURE. TWO OVERSIZE CLUB CHAIRS UPHOLSTERED IN MEXICAN *SERAPE* FABRIC ADD VIBRANT COLOR.

SANTA FE STYLE

 Critics used to call Santa Fe style and Santa Fe rooms mere fads, blips on the screen of Western design. After all, how could anything so ephemeral as coyotes howling at the moon, hand-carved jackrabbits with startled eyes, and technicolor wooden snakes coexist with a style born of ancient Pueblo culture?

While the style's trendier aspects may eventually be written off, it has an enduring eclecticism. A Victorian chest and a Charles Eames chair can look comfortably at home here. So can *Imari* porcelains and oriental rugs, African tapestries and ancient pottery vessels, lace curtains and brocade upholstery.

Discriminating minimalism is the style's hallmark. Beyond the dramatic front doors one often encounters a ladder. Once functional in Anasazi culture, ladders are now a decorative accessory for displaying woven blankets, jewelry, and rugs.

Bold plants—cactus, ficus, and bougainvillea—bring nature indoors. Tom-tom drums rest by the fireplace. Art ranges from ledger drawings and the Reubenesque women of an R.C. Gorman painting to Art Deco and works by early Taos artists. *Santos,* sculpture, baskets, and storytelling dolls give a sense of tradition. Earthenware, tin, brass, pewter, and silver serving dishes decorated with whimsical Western motifs, as well as furniture painted with tongue-in-cheek animal scenes, again reveal the Western sense of humor.

However simple or elegant the finished result of Santa Fe style may be, it is always unpretentious and understated, as inviting as the kind of "old friend" styles one finds in log cabins or old ranch houses.

ABOVE: DESIGNER CHARLES EAMES HELPED DEFINE THE MODERN LOOK OF AMERICAN FURNITURE DURING THE 1950S. HIS MOLDED-PLYWOOD-AND-LEATHER CHAIRS WERE THE EPITOME OF LUXURY AND SOPHISTICATION AND WERE COMMON ACCESSORIES FROM THE MIDWEST TO THE PACIFIC WEST. *OPPOSITE:* THE SITTING ROOM OF THE INN OF THE ANASAZI IN SANTA FE, NEW MEXICO, INVITES RELAXATION WITH AN OVERSTUFFED LEATHER SOFA, RUSTIC COFFEE TABLE, AND NAVAJO CHIEF'S BLANKET ON THE FLOOR. NATIVE AMERICAN-DESIGN DOORS ARE BY JEREMY MORRELLI OF SANTA FE.

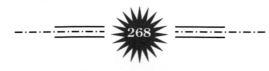

BELOW

MASTER CRAFTSMAN JEREMY MORRELLI OF SANTA FE, NEW MEXICO, PRODUCES A DISTINCTIVE LINE OF ENTRY DOORS IN "OLD WORLD" STYLES, INCLUDING THIS THRESHOLD WITH A FRONTIER LOOK THAT BLENDS WELL WITH SANTA FE ECLECTICISM.

ABOVE

A 1940S CAMP BLANKET, HEAVILY INFLUENCED BY THE NATIVE AMERICAN-INSPIRED DESIGNS OF PENDLETON MILLS OF OREGON, FINDS NEW LIFE COVERING A CHILD'S ROCKER. THE DESIGN IS BY SUSAN WUNDERLICH OF CHICAGO.

BELOW

FURNITURE DESIGNER SUSAN WUNDERLICH
OF CHICAGO HAS CREATED A UNIQUE
WESTERN LINE BY UPHOLSTERING ANTIQUE
FURNITURE WITH WESTERN-THEME TEXTILES.
THIS SMALL LADIES' CHAIR IS COVERED IN A
1950S CAMP BLANKET THAT EXPLOITS THE
FAMILIAR MOTIF OF INDIANS ON HORSEBACK.

ABOVE

THE INTERIOR OF A HOUSE IN THE CHIC VILLAGE OF TESUQUE,
NEW MEXICO, ON THE OUTSKIRTS OF SANTA FE BOASTS A WEALTH
OF SOUTHWESTERN ARTIFACTS. A MASSIVE TAOS DRUM TABLE, A
COLONIAL CHEST, AND NATIVE AMERICAN BUCKSKIN TREASURES ARE
THE HIGHLIGHTS OF THE ROOM.

LEFT

OUR LADY OF SORROWS, DEPICTED HERE BY NOTED *SANTERO* CHARLIE CARRILLO OF SANTA FE, NEW MEXICO, IS MARY AT THE HEIGHT OF HER PASSION AND SUFFERING DURING CHRIST'S CRUCIFIXION. OUR LADY OF SORROWS IS A FAVORITE PATRON SAINT OF NEW MEXICANS, AND SEVERAL CHURCHES ARE NAMED FOR HER.

BELOW

AN ANTIQUE CHIPPENDALE-STYLE SIDEBOARD IN SCULPTOR JOHN MORTENSEN'S WILSON, WYOMING, HOME IS ADORNED WITH A PANTHEON OF KACHINA DOLLS. OTHER RELICS OF THE OLD WEST AND THE SOUTHWEST, INCLUDING A BEADED POUCH, BUCKSKIN-AND-HOOF STOOL, AND CLASSIC NAVAJO RUG, COMPLETE THE COLLECTION.

ABOVE

A PAIR OF COLLECTIBLE "WOOLLY" CHAPS AND A LONGHORN CHAIR WITH COWHIDE UPHOLSTERY
ADD A RANCH TOUCH TO THIS SOUTHWESTERN ADOBE INTERIOR DECORATED IN THE
SANTA FE ECLECTIC STYLE.

CALIFORNIA LIFESTYLES

I f ever there is a design Eden, it has to be California. Anything goes. Everything seems right. Here in this fantasy land of slow time and movies, high tech and beaches, avant garde design thrives. California is a playful breeding ground of bold, exotic ideas.

From the historical Mission style with its timeless charm to the gleaming steel and glass of stark contemporary (once considered the antithesis of all things Western), California fosters design themes and a sun-centered lifestyle with seductive glamour and fantasy.

With a wealth of modern or abstract architectural styles defining California living, interiors complement those themes. Vaulted ceilings give interiors an expansive look, almost as if they were stretching to reach the sky. Windows usurp wall space. Interior finishes are often stucco or natural woods. Accents are provided by chrome and neon. Mirrors, the hallmark of Hollywood's Golden Age, are plentiful. High-tech touches abound.

With the Pacific Design Center in Los Angeles serving as an incubator for new ideas, California designers can draw from a palette of one-of-a-kind finishes for interiors, unusual fabrics, carpets, lighting, and accessories.

Increasingly, Asian and oriental influences are seen in these California expressions, blending with designs that still show the influence of Santa Fe styles and Frank Lloyd Wright themes. The result is a minimalist design style where less is more, making for a dramatic statement about the way Californians dress their homes.

ABOVE: IN THIS RANCHO MIRAGE HOME, ARCHITECT E. STEWART WILLIAMS USED GLASS, WOOD BEAMS, AND RIBBED CONCRETE BLOCKS TO ADD TEXTURAL CONTRAST TO THE OFF-WHITE FURNISHINGS. THE SEE-THROUGH FIREPLACE SERVES BOTH THE FORMAL LIVING ROOM AND ADJACENT FAMILY ROOM. *OPPOSITE:* ROUGH-HEWN BEAMS AND A GRANITE HEARTH CREATE A DRAMATIC HOME WITH A TRUE CALIFORNIA SPIRIT. THE RESIDENCE ALSO FUNCTIONS AS AN ART GALLERY FOR THE OWNER, WHO SERVES ON THE LOCAL MUSEUM BOARD.

LEFT

THIS RANCHO MIRAGE RESIDENCE WAS REMODELED BY INSIGHT TO TYPIFY THE STREAMLINED LOOK SO POPULAR IN CALIFORNIA HOMES. NEUTRAL WALLS AND FURNISHINGS ARE ACCENTED BY A RAUSCHENBERG PAINTING OVER THE FIREPLACE, A BLOWN-GLASS POT ON THE STEEL-AND-GLASS GAME TABLE, AND A COFFEE TABLE EMBELLISHED WITH NATIVE AMERICAN BEADWORK.

RIGHT

WORKING AT HOME TAKES ON NEW MEANING WHEN THE SETTING IS IN HOLLYWOOD HILLS. THE OFFICE OF THIS HOME, DESIGNED BY DENNIS HAGUE, OVERLOOKS A RUNNING BROOK AND A SWIMMING POOL. HEAVY BEAMED CEILINGS GIVE A RANCH FEELING TO THE ROOM, WHICH INCLUDES PERIOD FURNISHINGS, A RUG OF LEATHER STRIPS, AND A COFFEE TABLE MADE OF WROUGHT IRON AND AN OLD STONE WHEEL.

OPPOSITE

THIS PALM SPRINGS, CALIFORNIA, HOME BEGAN LIFE AS A GUEST HOUSE ON A LARGE ESTATE. THE EXTERIOR SUGGESTS A TYPICAL SMALL BUNGALOW, SURROUNDED BY WELL-TENDED GARDENS AND AN INVITING POOL. INSIDE, THE FEELING IS MEDITERRANEAN, WITH MOROCCAN INFLUENCES.

PACIFIC NORTHWEST STYLE

Think of bungalows, totem poles, and Tlingit baskets and you'll understand the style of the Pacific Northwest, which stretches from Oregon and Washington to Alaska. While all the typical vestiges of the West are represented here, the Pacific Northwest has been an atelier for the sculptural forms of Northwest Coast tribal art.

Woven in with all the other influences are carved ceremonial works of art. As author William C. Ketchum, Jr., explains, "The artists incorporated into their work the almost unrecognizable figures of animals such as Bear, Otter, Frog, Eagle, Killer Whale, Raven and Mountain Lion, who were believed to have supernatural powers that might be transferred to humans." Such designs have been carved into rattles, food bowls, dance masks, quirts, effigy columns, and house posts. Relics from Plains Indians and Chippewa snow shoes are other interior-design objects in the Pacific Northwest.

Baskets made by Tlingit women in southeastern Alaska are particularly valuable, according to basket authority Natalie Fay Linn of Portland, Oregon. Their popularity was ensured by the late 1800s, when Alaska was a favorite spot for collecting Indian basketware. Says Linn, "Travel companies promoted trips throughout Alaska to show Indians making baskets in their natural habitats."

If you're collecting baskets, look for an intentional flaw or break in the design. "Native American women did not strive to emulate perfection in their baskets," Linn notes. "They believed only the gods were allowed to be perfect, so each basket contained at least one tiny imperfection."

ABOVE: THIS A-FRAME ON PUGET SOUND, RENOVATED BY OLSON/SUNDBERG ARCHITECTS, REVEALS THE STRONG INFLUENCE OF ORIENTAL AND ASIAN ARCHITECTURAL AND DESIGN MOTIFS ON THE PACIFIC NORTHWEST. THE WATERSIDE RETREAT IS SET AGAINST A BACKDROP OF TALL PINES AND OTHER TREES INDIGENOUS TO THE AREA.

RIGHT: THIS INTERIOR VIEW OF THE RENOVATED CONTEMPORARY A-FRAME RETREAT NEAR SEATTLE SHOWS THE INFLUENCE OF PACIFIC NORTHWEST DESIGN THEMES. A TOTEM POLE STANDS GUARD ON THE DECK OVERLOOKING PUGET SOUND. WOOD WINDOWS WERE REPLACED WITH ALUMINUM BY OLSON/SUNDBERG ARCHITECTS. THE BUILDING'S ORIGINAL ARCHITECT WAS MARY LUND DAVIS.

LEFT

THE SPARE, SIMPLE DESIGN OF THIS
STAIRWAY BLENDS WOOD AND METAL FOR A
CONTEMPORARY APPROACH TO WESTERN
DESIGN. A LONG, VERTICAL WINDOW BRINGS
IN A SLIVER OF THE OUTDOORS. THE NATIVE
AMERICAN BASKET AND POTTERY ADD A
TOUCH OF TRADITION AND HISTORY TO
THE SETTING.

ABOVE

THIS BASKET OF SPRUCE ROOT AND BEAR
GRASS IS TYPICAL OF THOSE MADE BY THE
WOMEN OF THE TLINGIT NATION IN
SOUTHEASTERN ALASKA. OF THE 14 TLINGIT
TRIBES, THE YAKUTAT ARE CONSIDERED THE
MOST PROLIFIC BASKET MAKERS, CREATING
THIN-WALLED BASKETS, MOST OF WHICH
WERE USED FOR GATHERING BERRIES OR FOR
STEAMPOT COOKING.

LEFT

THIS HIGHLY COLLECTIBLE WILLOW-AND-DEVIL'S-CLAW BASKET, EMPLOYING VEGETABLE AND PLANT DYES, IS A TYPICAL NAVAJO WEDDING BASKET. NOTE THE FINISH BAND OF COILING AND ITS SLIGHT IMPERFECTIONS.

BELOW

THIS BOWL, TYPICAL OF THE HOPI-SIBYATKI TRIBES, IS REPRESENTATIVE OF POTTERY MADE AT A TIME WHEN INDIANS HAD HAD NO PREVIOUS CONTACT WITH EUROPEANS. THE BOWL USES THE STYLIZED THUNDERBIRD MOTIF FREQUENTLY FOUND IN NATIVE AMERICAN POTTERY.

ABOVE

THIS WOVEN LIDDED BASKET WITH ORNAMENTAL LEATHER STRIPS IS TYPICAL OF THE SALISH STYLE. WHILE THE TRIBE THAT MADE IT IS UNKNOWN, IT MAY HAVE BEEN ONE OF THE PLATEAU PEOPLES ALONG THE NORTHWEST COAST.

LEFT

This Pacific Northwest kitchen is a cook's stew of influences—the sleek lines of wood, glass, and steel suggest strong Asian design themes, while the dining chair has a hint of Gustav Stickley. Open shelves display Native American baskets and pottery.

LEFT

AN EXTENDED VIEW OF THE LIVING AND
DINING AREA IN THIS MAGNOLIA BLUFF
HOME SHOWS THE INFLUENCE OF ASIAN
ARCHITECTURE ON WESTERN DESIGN. A
WHITE-MARBLE FLOOR LENDS A SPACIOUS
MOOD TO THE ROOM, AS DO THE SLIDING
DOORS LEADING TO THE OUTSIDE GARDENS.
THE CEILING MIXES WOOD AND METAL FOR
CONTEMPORARY DRAMA. OLSON/SUNDBERG
ARCHITECTS CREATED THE ROOM
AS A PAVILION.

ABOVE

A CLASSIC MASONRY FIREPLACE SURROUNDED
BY WOOD IS THE FOCAL POINT OF THIS
GROUPING FROM THE SAME ROOM. A LIGHT
SOURCE COVERED BY FUSED GLASS ADDS
DRAMATIC INTEREST, AS DOES THE DIVERSE
COLLECTION OF NATIVE AMERICAN POTTERY.
THE COFFEE TABLE IS ACCENTED WITH
BRANCHES OF THE MADRONE TREE,
INDIGENOUS TO THE SEATTLE AREA.

ACCESSORIES WITH A WESTERN FLAIR

When *Metropolitan Home* magazine singled out a Molesworth-inspired couch covered with a Chimayo weaving as one of its top 100 designs in 1992, Western craftsmen knew they were onto something. The furnishings and accessories they had grown up with and loved for years had finally received national acclaim.

Consider, too, the companion list that was published that year in the *San Francisco Examiner* of design styles that were (and still are) in vogue: unprocessed wood, strong colors, bison skulls, wolves, Charlie Russell paintings, Pendleton blankets, weathered leather, and the venerable wagon wheel.

Whether the finishing touches we use to dress our homes in Western style are heirlooms passed down through the family, new finds gleaned from attics and estate sales, or reproductions and reinterpretations, the creators of those accessories all share a passionate love for the West, old and new.

Think of the Old West and you're likely to conjure up images of wagon trains and masked bandits, rodeos and gunfights at high noon. It's cowboys and corrals, whiskey and wild, wild women sashaying through the swinging doors of a saloon. But think of the New West and the most likely images are those being handcrafted by more than 500 enterprising artisans and entrepreneurs. These men and women are creating works of art and making sturdy home furnishings and accessories that have a contemporary spirit but with roots in the historical past.

These artists and craftsmen—from Montana to Massachusetts—are creating new classics that embrace the pioneer spirit, while reflecting the freshness of a new generation that is just discovering the beauty, mystique, and romance of the West. Dubbed today's "new pioneers," they are forging new trails as they honor history while establishing new standards for Western style.

However diverse their backgrounds and the works they produce, these artisans are all creating new Western icons. And like their ancestors, they are building traditions that will stand the test of time. Above all, these artists and craftsmen are not city slickers or dudes. They are lifetime cowboys and cowgirls who bring to their art an undying respect for the hard work and traditions that are synonymous with the Western lifestyle.

LEFT: FIFTEEN YEARS AGO, L.D. BURKE III GAVE UP THE CORPORATE LIFESTYLE AND HEADED FOR SANTA FE TO CREATE CONTEMPORARY HANDCRAFTED DERIVATIVES OF TRADITIONAL NEW MEXICAN FURNITURE. HIS PIECES ARE NOTED FOR HUMOROUS COWBOY SAYINGS THAT ARE SPELLED OUT ON HIS CREATIONS.

ABOVE: RON McGEE DESIGNED AND BUILT SANTA FE-STYLE HOMES IN PHOENIX BEFORE TURNING HIS LOVE OF FURNITURE BUILDING INTO A FULL-TIME CAREER. THIS METAL-AND-WOOD CHAIR WITH STAR CUTOUTS—PERFECT, PERHAPS, FOR A COUNTY SHERIFF—IS BASED ON A SIMPLE DESIGN.

BELOW: HAND-CARVED FURNISHINGS ARE THE FOCAL POINT OF THIS DINING ROOM, WHICH INCLUDES NUMEROUS WESTERN MOTIFS: HAND-PAINTED *VIGAS* ON THE CEILING, AN UNUSUAL CHANDELIER AND WALL SCONCES, AND COWBOY CHINA DISPLAYED IN THE HUTCH.

ABOVE: WILLIAM ACHEFF IS ONE OF THE WEST'S PREMIER CONTEMPORARY ARTISTS. HE BRINGS TO HIS ART A BACKGROUND RICH IN MULTICULTURAL INFLUENCES, INCLUDING HIS GEORGIAN AND ATHABASCAN INDIAN HERITAGE. HIS PHOTOREALISTIC STILL LIFES, LIKE THIS ONE ENTITLED *TULAROSA,* ARE KNOWN FOR INCORPORATING NATIVE AMERICAN POTTERY, DRUMS, BLANKETS, FETISHES, AND BEADED ARTIFACTS.

OPPOSITE: AN ADOBE BACKDROP, A FLAGSTONE PATIO, AND AN OLD WALL LANTERN ARE SIMPLE ACCOMPANIMENTS TO THIS DINING TABLE AND CHAIRS AT A SANTA FE, NEW MEXICO, RESIDENCE. CHRISTOPHER THOMSON IRONWORKS DESIGNED THE TABLE AND CHAIRS, WHICH REFLECT HIS TRADEMARK SIMPLE LINES AND GRACEFUL CURVES.

THE SOOTHING TOUCH OF LEATHER

eather is truly the hard worker of Western design. From a cowboy's boots and chaps to his saddle and holster, leather had to endure a rough lifestyle where weather and climate played no favorites.

Cowboys still must depend on leather as a companion on the trail. And anyone who has ever worn a pair of cowboy boots has a special feeling for them.

Collector Tyler Beard found cowboy boots so fascinating that he wrote an entire book about them, showing traditional styles made for real cowboys as well as those colorful fashion boots for cowboy wannabes. Bootmaking is still a time-honored tradition. At least two bootmakers, D.W. Fromer of Redmond, Oregon, and Dave Viers of Livingston, Montana, are making boots the old-fashioned way. Many factories and individuals are noted for custom boots: Paul Bond, Dean Jackson, Jay Griffith, Bill Crary, Dan Wells, D.L. McKinney, and James Leddy. There's even a boot-making school in Okmulgee, Oklahoma.

Early-day cowboys would probably be surprised to see cowboy boots used now as interior-design accents, marching across mantels, placed casually by the hearth or the bed, or used as a lamp base. They'd probably

ABOVE: PEEWEE-STYLE MEN'S COWBOY BOOTS FROM THE '40S OR '50S. *OPPOSITE:* MEN'S DRESS-UP BOOTS.

also smile on seeing saddles—plain, hand-tooled, embossed, or glitzed with silver *conchos*—placed dominantly in a room, the same way one might showcase an English armoire or highboy. Saddles were cowboys' most expensive gear, making them great collectibles today. That's a fact not lost on contemporary saddlemakers, especially Slim Green of Santa Fe, who has been making them for six decades.

Gary and Chris Galusha specialize in classic and contemporary leatherwork in their Santa Fe studio. Each piece they make is inspired by the artistic and historical legacy of the West. Karl Hipp of Redstone, Colorado, has forged a reputation by making original steel lamps in Western motifs with genuine rawhide shades.

Leather furnishings have long been synonymous with Western style. From the first primitive chairs with a strip of leather for a seat and back to today's plush versions, leather in all its forms and styles exudes the charm of the West.

RIGHT

THIS SILVER-MOUNTED PARADE SADDLE WAS MADE BY BRYBEN BROTHERS SADDLERY IN LOS ANGELES IN THE 1930S FOR TEDDY ARROGONE, A MEMBER OF THE LOS ANGELES COUNTY SHERIFF'S POSSE. IT FEATURES A SHERIFF'S STAR ON THE *TAPADEROS*. ARROGONE USED THIS SADDLE WHEN HE RODE WITH TOM MIX IN THE PASADENA ROSE BOWL PARADE. IT IS NOW OWNED BY GEORGE PITTMAN OF SAN GABRIEL, CALIFORNIA.

BELOW

THIS HAND-TOOLED SILVER-MOUNTED PARADE SADDLE IN BLACK LEATHER WAS MADE BY EDWARD BOHLIN IN THE 1930S. NOW OWNED BY WILLIAM MANNS OF SANTA FE, NEW MEXICO, THE SADDLE WAS PURCHASED BY ITS SECOND OWNER AT A GARAGE SALE IN IDAHO FOR $15. ITS VALUE TODAY IS APPROXIMATELY $12,000.

OPPOSITE

THIS SLICK FORK, LOOP-SEAT LEATHER STOCK SADDLE WAS MADE BY OTTO EVERS OF FREDERICKSBURG, TEXAS, AROUND THE TURN OF THE CENTURY. IT FEATURES A SQUARE SKIRT AND BORDER STAMP DECORATION WITH A WINCHESTER RIFLE SCABBARD. THIS CLASSIC COWBOY SADDLE IS NOW OWNED BY JOE GISH OF FREDERICKSBURG.

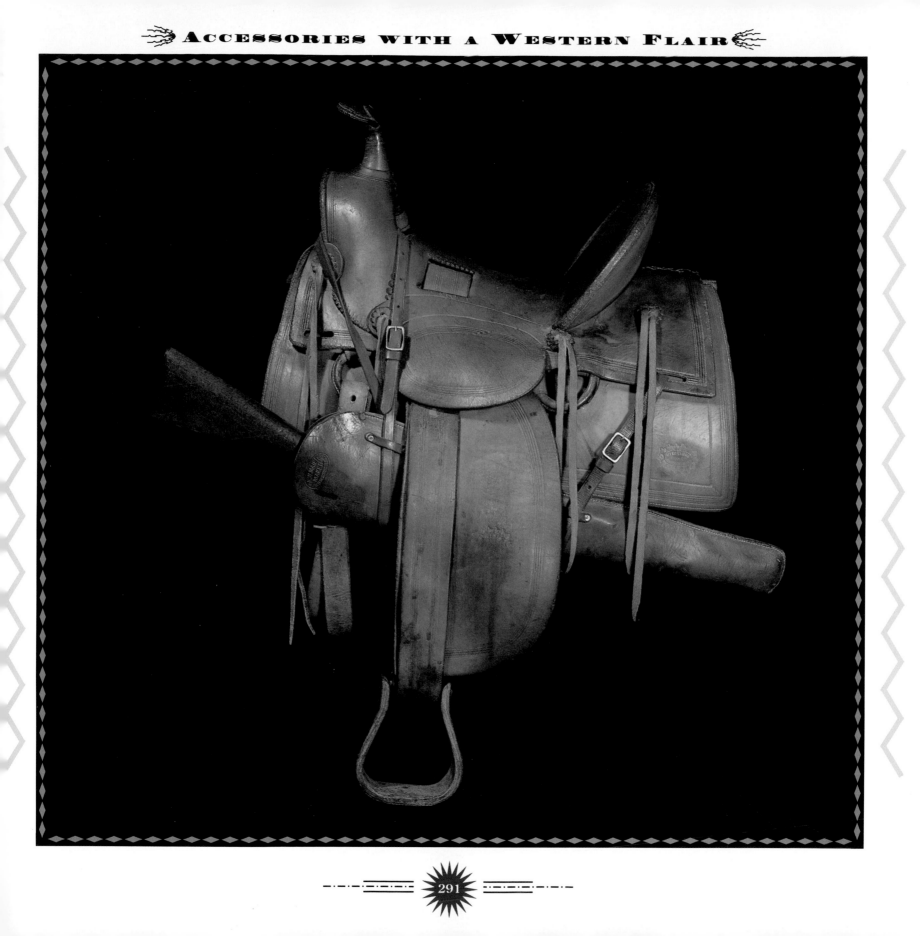

AS THE IRON IS WROUGHT

The blacksmith was as important as the town doctor or the traveling preacher in the early days of the West. He made everything from tools, spurs, and miners' tins to andirons, ranch signs, and gates. The furnishings of the West would be far different today had there been no blacksmiths.

Then consider the lowly tin can. The U.S. Army surely had little idea that the simple act of bringing tin cans to New Mexico in the late 1800s would give rise to an American folk-art form. Tin cans have become humble works of art: chandeliers, candle sconces and holders, lanterns, frames, trinket boxes, all manner of crosses, crowns for *santos, nichos* for religious art. Even today, tin roofs are an important architectural feature on Territorial and some Ranch-style homes.

According to *New Mexican Tinwork 1840-1940,* tin was considered so valuable in the mid-1800s that Brigham Young counseled his followers to bring along sheets of high-quality tin, as it "was better here than gold."

Examples of tinwork and that of the early blacksmith's efforts are favorite collectibles today. Equally prized are the works of artists using metal and tin for contemporary accessories.

Bert and Judy Hopple work from their log cabin in Wapiti, Wyoming, creating steel art and sand carving on glass, wood, and stone. When Cali-

ABOVE: ARTISAN GARY BLANK DESIGNED THIS HAND-PUNCHED TIN MIRROR WITH AN INTERIOR FRAME OF ENAMELED GLASS.
OPPOSITE: PUNCHED-TIN INLAYS BY BLANK ENHANCE WHITE-PINE KITCHEN CABINETS.

fornian Tony Alvis isn't working as an outfitter, he uses his blacksmith talents to make fireplace screens, chandeliers, lanterns, and wall hangings. John Mortensen of Wilson, Wyoming, makes rustic furnishings, each piece having a distinctive signed foundry casting. Many designers are using metal for dining tables and chairs, with interpretations that lean toward oriental and Roman styles.

Mike Livingston of Hutchinson, Kansas, designs unusual chandeliers that are like an interesting three-ring Western circus hovering over the dining table. Terry and Sandy Winchell of Fighting Bear Antiques, Jackson, Wyoming, use cowboy, Indian, and wildlife motifs for switch plates, nostalgic sconces, even toilet-paper holders. True West Designs in Clackamas, Oregon, does a take-off on the traditional torch with the metal silhouette of an Indian on his horse.

These simple touches of metal and tin, whether salvaged from the past or newly crafted, can go a long way to lend a Western mood to any room. It's also an easy way to whet your appetite for Western collecting.

SCENES FROM AN OLD WEST CATTLE DRIVE WERE THE INSPIRATION FOR THIS MODERN TABLE LAMP DESIGNED BY PAT OLSON. FASHIONED OF QUARTER-INCH PLATE STEEL, THE 18-INCH-HIGH LAMP DEPICTS A COWBOY HERDING HIS CATTLE TO MARKET. A RAWHIDE LAMP SHADE BOUND WITH LEATHER STRIPS CASTS A WARM GLOW IN ANY WESTERN SETTING.

ABOVE

JOHN MORTENSEN'S RAINBOW TRAIL COLLECTION IS ARTFULLY DISPLAYED IN FURNISHINGS TYPICAL OF THE CONTEMPORARY RUGGED STYLE IN WESTERN FURNISHINGS. EACH PIECE FEATURES A FOUNDRY CASTING SIGNED BY THE ARTIST. THE SILHOUETTES OF WESTERN ICONS ARE AS EFFECTIVE FOR CHAIR BACKS AND BOOKENDS AS THEY ARE FOR ANDIRONS AND LAMP AND TABLE BASES.

ABOVE

THIS BUFFALO-HUNT CHANDELIER MIXES MANY OF THE TRADITIONAL MATERIALS OF WESTERN DESIGN, PARTICULARLY RAWHIDE AND METAL. THE PAINTED FIGURES ON THE TEPEE SUGGEST ANCIENT NATIVE AMERICAN SYMBOLS, AS DO THE SKULLS AND ARROWS THAT MARCH UP THE SYMBOLIC TEPEE-SHAPED IRONWORK. AN INDIAN PERPETUALLY HERDS THE BUFFALO AROUND THE RIM OF THE LAMP.

OPPOSITE

BRONZE SCULPTOR JOHN MORTENSEN IS SHOWN AT WORK IN THE STUDIO OF HIS WILSON, WYOMING, HOME. THE LOG-CABIN STUDIO IS AN INSPIRING SETTING FOR HIM TO CREATE HIS COWBOY AND WILDLIFE SCULPTURES AND FURNISHINGS. NAVAJO RUGS ABOUND, AS DO STUFFED WILDLIFE, HORNS, AND COWBOY HATS. THERE'S EVEN AN OLD RAWHIDE SHADE LAMP ON THE DROP-LEAF TABLE.

MEXICAN TILE AND HARDWARE

Two signatures of Western design—Mexican tile and hardware—are ornamentations found especially throughout the Southwest. Tiles cover floors and counters, dance around fireplaces, line swimming pools, and march across steps. Tiles mix function with beauty, introducing color, a smooth-as-glass finish, and visual interest. Hardware is the final touch on *trasteros* and cupboards, chests and cabinets; it's as important to furniture as buttons are to fashion.

Saltillo—those large terra cotta squares—is favored for floors and makes an excellent background for area rugs and furnishings. Blue is a popular tile color in Western kitchens, with varying shades often forming unusual and random patterns. Like many other aspects of Western design, tiles tell miniature stories, as if they were creating a comic strip in ceramic. Some are odes to the changing seasons, while others share insights into ethnic traditions.

ABOVE: THIS WESTERN DOOR IS FASHIONED FROM SPLIT LOGS STILL DRESSED IN THEIR ORIGINAL BARK. THE DOOR HANDLES OF OLD IRON ARE ACCENTED WITH VARIOUS SIZES OF HORSESHOES, PERHAPS TO BRING GOOD LUCK TO THOSE WHO STEP INSIDE.

Early hardware was always crude—like the wrought-iron latches and locks that secured food stores, clothing, and household treasures. While hardware still has tough work to do, contemporary artisans, especially Peter Fillerup of Heber, Utah, have softened the rustic, handmade look, elevating hardware to a form of art.

Sometimes hardware is fashioned of the wood itself; other times the hardware derives from Western trappings—like the horseshoes that Tom and Maril Bice of Longmont, Colorado, use on hand-hewn log cupboards, or the metal stars on wood and stained-glass furnishings by the Eccentric Western Furniture Company of Bozeman, Montana.

Such hardware is not only functional but a much-sought-after collectible. Hardware now is even considered an accessory. Grouped together as a decorative element on a white stucco wall, hardware items add texture—and, as always, invite conversation.

ABOVE: THE INFLUENCE OF EARLY ADIRONDACK FURNISHINGS IS EXPRESSED IN THIS TEAK FURNITURE GROUPING THAT GRACES A WESTERN PATIO. THE SHAPES ARE SPARE AND SIMPLISTIC, YET GRACEFUL. THE SOFT COLOR OF THE WOOD COMPLEMENTS THE TERRA COTTA TILES OF THE PATIO FLOOR.

BELOW

RON JONES, OWNER OF SIERRA CUSTOM HOMES IN SANTA FE, NEW MEXICO, CREATED THIS PATIO SETTING FOR AN AVID GARDENER AT HIS HOME IN THE LA TIERRA AREA NEAR SANTA FE. LUSH PLANTINGS, PINE TREES, AND NATIVE GRASSES ARE SET AGAINST THIS BLUE CERAMIC TILE BACKDROP, WHICH FEATURES A TERRA COTTA SUN GOD EMBELLISHED WITH A MOSAIC OF COLORFUL CERAMIC TILES.

ABOVE

OLD WROUGHT-IRON HARDWARE CAN GO A LONG WAY TOWARD MAKING A DRAMATIC STATEMENT ABOUT WESTERN STYLE. THESE HINGES AND DRAWER PULLS WERE MADE BY EARLY-DAY BLACKSMITHS USING SIMPLE· TOOLS. THEY ARE SHOWN AGAINST A BACKGROUND OF LEATHER CHAPS. A FELT COWBOY HAT WITH A RAWHIDE BAND IS SHOWN AT THE TOP.

ABOVE

THIS ADOBE ARCHWAY LEADING TO A SOUTHWESTERN PATIO IS ENHANCED BY THE WHIMSICAL IRON GATE CREATED BY CHRISTOPHER THOMSON IRONWORKS. THE DESIGN IS SIMPLE YET IMAGINATIVE. THE GRACEFUL CURVES SUGGEST EYES THAT ARE EVER WATCHFUL OF ALL WHO PASS THROUGH THIS PORTAL.

OPPOSITE

THE MASTER BEDROOM OF THIS MONATANA RESIDENCE IS A SANCTUARY OF QUIET WESTERN ELEGANCE. AN OLD MONASTERY DOOR, WITH ITS HEAVY ANTIQUE HARDWARE AND IRON KEY STILL IN PLACE, OPENS TO A FOYER SETTING WHERE WESTERN ARTIFACTS BECOME OBJECTS OF ART.

THE NEW LOOK IN WESTERN FINE ART

The longing to reach a higher truth, which we associate with the great painters and sculptors of old, is true of contemporary Western artists who are heralding a new style. It is a form evolving from early illustrative traditions to works that now find their inspiration in preserving the West of today in unusual, more modern forms. Where Western art used to provide an excellent history lesson for those who liked art mixed with nostalgia, it is now a history lesson presented through the prism of the present. Whether the artist is representing the intricacies of a Navajo wool harvest or painting sunflowers or snow, there is the sense that, as viewers and collectors, we are experiencing the West as it is today.

Walt Gonske paints bold impressionist portraits of northern New Mexico, his canvases thick with the unique color and texture of the mountains. William E. Matthews and Nelson Boren present emotionally moving vignettes of the cowboy lifestyle, rather than full-scale Western scenes. Scott Christensen paints impressionistic landscapes—the Oregon coast, Jackson Hole—with a reserved sensitivity to nature.

Donna Howell-Sickles creates vivid paintings of women in the West, bringing in humor and challenging

ABOVE: THIS CERAMIC BASKET BY JIM KRAFT EXPRESSES ALL THE EARTHINESS OF THE SOUTHWEST.

stereotypes. Shirley Thomson-Smith offers a sculptor's perspective on Navajo women, her female forms always in a brooding posture.

James Reynolds and Bill Owens paint real cowboys at work in the West, much the same way Christopher Marona, Bob Moorhouse, and David Stoecklein photograph similar scenes from ranch life.

Wilson Hurley is known for expansive, cloud-filled skies and panoramic landscapes in monumental oil paintings. Steve Kestrel is influenced by the Southwest's vast, primeval landscapes. He lets stones—granite, schist, riverstone—dictate sculptures with an environmental message.

Contemporary Western artists bring a diversity of backgrounds to their work—some have been coaches, pilots, engineers, movie illustrators, designers, or architects on their way to the canvas or the sculptor's bench. Still, all are united in their love of the West and their appreciation of honest, authentic craftsmanship.

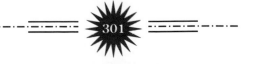

LEFT: WESTERN ARTIST FREDERIC REMINGTON OFTEN SCULPTED MINIATURES OF SUBJECTS FOR HIS PAINTINGS SO HIS PORTRAYALS WOULD BE AUTHENTIC. THIS BURRO, LADEN WITH A HEAVY LOAD AND HEADING UP A STEEP MOUNTAIN, IS CAST AGAIN IN MANY OF REMINGTON'S COMPELLING SCENES AND SCULPTURES OF THE OLD WEST.

LEFT

BILL OWEN'S OIL PAINTING, *BRUSH HANDS WAITING FOR DAYLIGHT,* IS AN HONEST PORTRAYAL OF THE COWBOY LIFESTYLE. "BRUSH HANDS" IS A COMMON TERM FOR COWBOYS WHO WORK IN ROUGH, BRUSHY COUNTRY, LIKE THIS SETTING IN ARIZONA. SAYS OWEN, IT TAKES "A SPECIAL KIND OF HORSE AND COWBOY TO WORK WILD CATTLE." THESE COWBOYS HAVE RIDDEN OUT IN THE EARLY MORNING AND BUILT A FIRE TO WARM UP WHILE DISCUSSING THE COMING DAY'S WORK.

RIGHT

ARIZONA COWBOYS BY ARIZONA ARTIST JAMES E. REYNOLDS REFLECTS HIS FAVORITE THEME, THE ROLE OF HORSES IN A COWBOY'S WORK AND THE AFFINITY A COWBOY FEELS FOR HIS HORSE. THE PAINTING WON THE PRESTIGIOUS PRIX DE WEST AWARD IN 1992 FROM THE NATIONAL COWBOY HALL OF FAME. A FORMER HOLLYWOOD SCENE DESIGNER, REYNOLDS MOVED TO ARIZONA IN 1968 TO PURSUE HIS LIFELONG DREAM OF PAINTING THE WEST.

RIGHT

WILLIAM MATTHEWS'S PAINTING, *STAMPEDE STRING*, IS HIS REALISTIC VIEWPOINT OF THE COWBOY LIFESTYLE. MATTHEWS IS DRAWN TO THE DUSTY TRAILS AND VAST OPEN SPACES OF THE WEST, BUT HE IS NOT MERELY AN ARMCHAIR OBSERVER. HE HAS BUNKED WITH WORKING COWBOYS AT SOME OF THE BEST RANCHES IN THE WEST, SHARED MEALS WITH THEM, CINCHED UP A SADDLE, AND TIED DOWN STEERS IN BLINDING SNOWSTORMS.

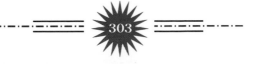

WHIMSICAL WESTERN-STYLE ACCESSORIES

Everybody knows that cowboys have always loved a good laugh. Sitting around the campfire after a long day on the trail, cowboys could count on a well-told tale with a good punch line—albeit sometimes raucous and off-color. Laughter, hearty or subdued, is part of the music of the West.

Whimsy and humor take form in many ways, going well beyond those wooden coyotes howling at the moon. Furniture made from burled roots and twigs always has a certain offbeat humor to it.

Even lodgepole pine can bring a chuckle. Gary Phillips of Tetonia, Idaho, who founded The Drawknife, a furniture and accessory company, in 1980, says he has always taken pleasure in seeing furniture that was "bug-tracked, curved, fire-scarred, or just unusually formed."

Jake Lemon of Sun Valley, Idaho, has "no taste for glitz" and goes instead for quiet smiles, not guffaws.

His furnishings are inspired by the romantic ski resorts of the 1930s and '40s: "One should be able to see Ernest Hemingway, Averell Harriman, and Gary Cooper leaning back with their feet up on this stuff."

ABOVE: JERRY ENGLAND MAKES WHIMSICAL WESTERN-STYLE FURNISHINGS.

Californian Jerry England's cowboy-chic designs, marketed under the "Lure of the Dim Trails" label, is folk-art furniture and accessories at their best, custom made with relief or scratch-carved gunfighters, cowboys, Indians, and wildlife. It's only natural, says England, that he should be making cowboy furnishings with a dash of humor and fantasy.

Then there's L.D. Burke of Santa Fe, known for his whimsical furnishings—from bedsteads to *trasteros,* lightly distressed with a flail, all incorporating the traditional artifacts of the cowboy lifestyle: bits, bridles, stirrups, spurs, sheriff's badges, arrows, knives, and guns. Burke is also famous for humorous, cowboy-style sayings that are etched, burned, or studded into his creations.

"The sayings just pop into my head," he confesses. Like his counterparts, Burke is building furniture to last—"at least for three generations."

Call it making furniture the cowboy way.

ABOVE: WHO NEEDS A LULLABYE WHEN YOU'VE GOT SWEET DREAMS—WESTERN STYLE—HOVERING OVERHEAD? THIS HEADBOARD BY L.D. BURKE HAS A MESSAGE FASHIONED OF HORSESHOES. SPURS DECORATE THE BEDPOSTS.

BELOW: THIS MIRROR BY BURKE FEATURES AN OLD SPANISH SAYING AND IS ADORNED WITH A SPUR AT THE TOP. IN THE MIRROR ARE REFLECTIONS OF OTHER MIRRORS MADE BY THIS SANTA FE ARTISAN.

ABOVE: JERRY ENGLAND IS KNOWN FOR MAKING WESTERN FURNITURE THAT MIXES HISTORY WITH HUMOR. WHAT CHILD WOULDN'T LOVE A CHEST ADORNED WITH HORSEHEADS AND BUCKING BRONCOS AND A MIRROR OUTLINED WITH SOME OF THE WEST'S MOST FAMOUS BRANDS? *INSET:* THIS CUSTOM TABLE BY ENGLAND FEATURES AN UNUSUAL TABLETOP DETAIL. METAL WESTERN FIGURES PARADE AROUND IT, WHILE EMBLEMS OF THE WEST—A GUN, HOLSTER, SPUR AND U.S. MARSHAL'S BADGE— ADORN THE TOP.

COLLECTIBLES, FROM COWBOY KITSCH TO SERIOUS STUFF

Just about anything can attract a collector's fancy. Some people collect rodeo china, miner's carbide lamps and cottonwood *santos*. Others adore Route 66 trinkets and Lone Ranger rings. What seems ridiculous to one person may be a full-fledged passion to someone else.

What does one collect to express the Western personality? The choice depends on your own style. Cowboy-hat and *sombrero* ashtrays were popular during the 1940s and '50s. Made of copper, silver, tin, terra cotta, glass, or porcelain, they occasionally carried imprints of casinos, hotels, restaurants, or rodeos. Costing anywhere from $2 to $25, they're great fun for novice collectors.

Cowboy spurs and saddles are two popular collectibles. Spurs helped cowboys control wayward horses; they were also a status symbol. Made of cast or wrought iron, nickel, silver, copper, brass, or stainless steel, they were often heavily embossed or engraved with silver mountings. Like chaps and hats, these too had regional trademarks. Writes William C. Ketchum, Jr., author of *Collecting the West,* "A maker's mark will always enhance the value of a set of spurs." The same goes for saddlemaking, Ketchum adds, noting that Edward Bohlin of Hollywood, California, was known for elaborate tooling, silver conchos, and cast-silver plates with incised figures of cowboys, horses, and cattle. One-of-a-kind pieces like Bohlin's will fetch high prices.

ABOVE: ROBERT BRANDES OF AUSTIN, TEXAS, HAS AN EXTENSIVE BUCKLE COLLECTION. THIS TROPHY-STYLE BUCKLE WAS MADE IN 1940.

Richard Rattenbury, curator of history for the National Cowboy Hall of Fame in Oklahoma City, sees guns and gunleather as valuable collectibles. "Colt revolvers and Winchester rifles have become icons of our frontier mythos," says Rattenbury.

Beadwork is a traditional form of embellishment in Native American cultures, dressing up moccasins, cradleboards, pipe bags, and horse blankets. Tribal differences can be denoted by beadwork styles. Some tribes continue these old traditions.

Cast-silver jewelry is highly prized. Jewelry made by Native American silversmiths reflects tribal distinctions—simple designs, massive forms by Navajos; heavy inlays of turquoise and other stones by Zunis; overlays and cutwork by Hopis.

Kachinas have their basis in the Hopi and Zuni spirit world and are small figures carved from cottonwood roots. Collectors value those that are trimmed with shells, feathers, straw, cloth, and leather.

ABOVE: THIS COWBOY CHINA FROM THE NATIONAL COWBOY HALL OF FAME IS PERFECT FOR LITTLE BUCKAROOS WHO MIGHT BALK AT CLEANING UP THEIR PLATE. BRANDS CIRCLE THE PLATE AND CUP; A YOUNG COWBOY RIDES ACROSS THE PLATE'S CORRAL. A FRIENDLY GREETING GRACES THE BOTTOM OF THE CEREAL BOWL. *TOP LEFT:* MUCH OF THE LORE OF THE WEST IS PRESERVED IN OLD SONGBOOKS THAT REVEAL THE LIFESTYLE OF COWBOYS ON EARLY RANCHES. SINGING SONGS IN THE BUNKHOUSE OR AROUND THE CAMPFIRE WAS A ROUTINE PART OF THE DAY. *BOTTOM LEFT:* FICTION ABOUT THE WEST FOUND A READY HOME IN EARLY-DAY PULP MAGAZINES, WHICH WERE ILLUSTRATED BY SOME OF THE COUNTRY'S FINEST WESTERN ARTISTS. MANY EVENTUALLY TURNED TO FINE-ART CAREERS AS THE PULP MARKET FADED. *TOP RIGHT:* THESE SILVER SPURS FEATURE ORNATE HAND TOOLING OF A COWBOY ON A BUCKING HORSE, RUBY INSETS, AND A PATRIOTIC SHIELD DECORATION. THE ROWELS ARE SILVER. *BOTTOM RIGHT:* THIS SIX-SHOOTER IS SIMILAR TO COLT .44-CALIBER SINGLE-ACTION STYLES. THE LEATHER HOLSTER FEATURES A CITY MARSHAL BADGE.

ARTISTS:

William Acheff
P.O. Box 1036
Taos, New Mexico 87571
(505) 776-8513

James Bama
c/o Big Horn Gallery
1167 Sheridan Avenue
Cody, Wyoming 82414
(307) 527-7587

Jim Barnaby
Neo Cowboy Eccentric Western
     Furniture
P.O. Box 203
Bozeman, Montana 59771
(406) 587-3585

Nelson Boren
6000 Shingle Mill Road
Sand Point, Idaho 83864
(208) 265-4213

Charlie Carrillo
2712 Paseo de Tularosa
Santa Fe, New Mexico 87505
(505) 473-7941

Scott Christensen
P.O. Box 20096
Jackson, Wyoming 83001
(307) 733-5851

Michael Coleman
2822 Rolling Knolls Drive
Provo, Utah 84604
(801) 375-1259

Walt Gonske
P.O. Box 1538
Taos, New Mexico 87571
(505) 758-4042

Donna Howell-Sickles
Contemporary Southwest Galleries
123 West Palace Avenue
Santa Fe, New Mexico 87501
(505) 986-0440

Wilson Hurley
237 Spring Creek Court NE
Albuquerque, New Mexico
(505) 856-6537

Steve Kestrel
2604 Terrylake Road
Fort Collins, Colorado
(303) 482-9418

William C. Matthews
William Matthews Gallery
1617 Wazee Street
Denver, Colorado 80202
(303) 534-1300

Bill Owen
P.O. Box 490
Dewey, Arizona 86327
(602) 632-5320

James E. Reynolds
7760 East Gainey Ranch Road,
     No. 15
Scottsdale, Arizona 85258
(602) 443-8168

Shirley Thomson-Smith
2528 NW 59th Street
Oklahoma City, Oklahoma 73112
(405) 848-7243

Harold Joe Waldrum
Belen, New Mexico
(505) 864-4315
also:
  c/o Lumina of New Mexico
239 Morada Lane
Taos, New Mexico 87571
(505) 758-7282

COLLECTIBLES:

Tyler Beard (boots)
True West
Goldthwaithe, Texas 76844
(915) 648-2696

Robert R. Brandes (buckles)
P.O. Box 5808
Austin, Texas 78763
(512) 327-7366

Joe Gish (saddles)
502 North Milam
Fredericksburg, Texas 78624
(210) 997-2794

Ralph Kylloe (furniture)
Ralph Kylloe Antiques
298 High Range Road
Londonderry, New Hampshire 03053
(603) 437-2920

Natalie Fay Linn (baskets)
4125 SW 53rd Avenue
Portland, Oregon 97221
(503) 292-1711

DEALERS:

Hyde Park Antiques, Ltd.
836 Broadway
New York, New York 10003
(212) 477-0033

L. & J.G. Stickley, Inc.
P.O. Box 480
Manlius, New York 13104
(315) 682-5500

Ritter Antik
35 East 10th Street
New York, New York 10003
(212) 673-2213

Summer Hill, Ltd.
2682H Middlefield Road
Redwood City, California 94063
(415) 363-2600

DESIGNERS/ARCHITECTS/BUILDERS:

Adolf deRoy-Mark & Associates
Grapevine Horizon Drive
Carefree, Arizona 85377
(602) 488-2216

Alpine Log Homes
Main Street
Victor, Montana 59875
(406) 642-3461

Anderson, Koch & Smith
119 South Main, Suite 400
Seattle, Washington 98104
(206) 263-6832

Jeffrey Balch/Arcus Design Group
103 High Street
Westchester, Pennsylvania 19382
(215) 344-0909

Big Timberworks, Inc.
P.O. Box 368
Gallatin Gateway, Montana 59730
(406) 763-4639

J. Scott Carter
Wylie Carter Architects
16116 Northfield Street
Pacific Palisades, California 90272
(310) 459-7989

Charles Stuhlberg Interior Design
P.O. Box 629
Sun Valley, Idaho 83353
(208) 726-4568

Custom Log Homes
Drawer 226
Stevensville, Montana 59870
(406) 777-5202

Dennis Hague & Associates
8271 Melrose Avenue
Los Angeles, California 90046
(213) 653-4700

Dorman/Breen Architects
1524 Paseo de Peralta
Santa Fe, New Mexico 87501
(505) 982-9196

John Douglas
Douglas Architecture & Planning
7522 East McDonald
Scottsdale, Arizona 85252
(602) 951-2242

Ed Fitzgerald, Architect
2225 Lead Avenue SE
Albuquerque, New Mexico 85716
(505) 268-9055

Gamelsky, Benton Architects
622 Tijeras Avenue NW
Albuquerque, New Mexico 87102
(505) 842-8865

Garland Homes
P.O. Box 12
Victor, Montana 59875
(406) 642-3095

Garrett Smith, Ltd., Architect
514 Central Avenue SW
Albuquerque, New Mexico 87102
(505) 766-6968

Hasbrook Interiors & Antiques
7017 East Main Street
Scottsdale, Arizona 85251
(602) 994-1993

Holmes Sabatini Architects
202 Central SE, West Courtyard
Albuquerque, New Mexico 87102
(505) 247-3705

Insight West
45-125 Panorama
Palm Desert, California 92260
(619) 568-9089

Jean Steinbrecher, Architect
P.O. Box 788
Langley, Washington 98260
(360) 221-0494

Jon Anderson Architect AIA
912 Roma Avenue NW
Albuquerque, New Mexico 87102
(505) 764-8306

Ron Jones
Sierra Custom Homes
P.O. Box 7157
Albuquerque, New Mexico 87194

Kevin McKee & Associates
200 North Fourth, Suite 30
Boise, Idaho 83702
(208) 342-3300

Nancy Kitchell
Kitchell Interior Design Associates
7522 East McDonald, Suite C
Scottsdale, Arizona 85250
(602) 951-0280

Nancy Lippman
Lippman Entertainment
Beverly Hills, California
(310) 657-1500

Locati Architects
402 East Main Street, Suite 202
Bozeman, Montana 59715
(406) 587-1139

McHugh, Lloyd ,Tryk Architects
301 North Guadalupe, Suite 201
Santa Fe, New Mexico 87501
(505) 988-9789

McLaughlin Architecture
118 East Main
Bozeman, Montana 59715
(406) 586-0033

McPhie Cabinetry
435 East Main
Bozeman, Montana 59715
(406) 586-1708

Mongerson-Wunderlich
704 North Wells Street
Chicago, Illinois 60610
(312) 943-2354

Montana Log Homes
3212 Highway 93 South
Kalispell, Montana 59901
(406) 752-2992

Morrow, Bowden Architects
333 Montezuma Street
Santa Fe, New Mexico 87501
(505) 983-3755

Mortensen Designs, Inc.
P.O. Box 746
Wilson, Wyoming 83014
(307) 733-1519

Morter Architects
143 East Meadows Drive
Crossroads at Vail
Vail, Colorado 81657
(303) 476-5106

James D. Morton, AIA
2000 Jackson Creek Road
Bozeman, Montana 59715
(406) 587-2850

Jackie Mowry, ASID
7001 Montgomery Boulevard NE
Albuquerque, New Mexico 87109
(505) 881-9595

Nance Construction, Inc.
3601 East Marlette
Paradise Valley, Arizona 85253
(602) 224-0785

Nick Berman Design
1301 Tigertail Road
Los Angeles, California 90049
(310) 476-6342

Northwoods Log Homes
HCR 70, P.O. Box 645
La Porte, Minnesota 56461
(218) 224-2251

Old Style Log Works
P.O. Box 255
Kalispell, Montana 59901
(406) 892-4665

Olson/Sundberg Architects
108 First Avenue South, 4th Floor
Seattle, Washington 98104
(206) 624-5670

Paula Berg Design Associates, Inc.
7522 East McDonald
Scottsdale, Arizona 85250
(602) 998-2344

Robert W. Peters, FAIA
One Loop One NW
Albuquerque, New Mexico 87120
(505) 899-0454

Phil Korell, Architect
1538 Meadowlark Drive
Great Falls, Montana 59404
(406) 452-7004

Reichstetter Construction
P.O. Box 460
Big Sky, Montana 59716
(406) 587-8900

Rocky Mountain Habitats, Inc.
P.O. Box 1660
Bigfork, Montana 59911
(406) 862-5597

Jon Sayler, AIA
South 414 Thor
Spokane, Washington 99202
(509) 435-9207

Talbert/Malmquist Construction
P.O. Box 848
Whitefish, Montana 59937
(406) 862-7848

Timberhouse Post & Beam
150 Sheafman Creek Road
Victor, Montana 59875
(406) 961-3276

Timberpeg Construction
P.O. Box 5474
West Lebanon, New Hampshire
03784
(603) 298-8820

Julia Tometz
Tometz Design Associates, Inc.
747 North Oakwood Avenue
Lake Forest, Illinois 60045
(708) 295-5090

Kent Trauernicht
55 Camino del Senador
Tijeras, New Mexico 87059
(505) 281-9560

Warren Sheets Design
2017 17th Street
San Francisco, California 94103
(415) 626-2320

E. Stewart Williams
1250 Paseo el Mirador
Palm Desert, California 92262
(619) 327-3702

Wiseman & Gale
P.O. Box 1648
4015 North Marshall Way
Scottsdale, Arizona 85252
(602) 945-8447

Neil Wright
Wright, Bryant & Johnson, Inc.
P.O. Box 21
Sun Valley, Idaho 83353
(208) 726-4434

Tom Wuelpern
Rammed Earth Solar Homes, Inc.
265 West 18th Street, Suite 3
Tucson, Arizona 85701
(602) 623-2784

FURNITURE MAKERS:

Arizona Ranch
1300A East 8th Street
Tempe, Arizona 85281
(602) 921-1101

Arte de Mexico
1000 Chestnut Street
Burbank, California 91506
(818) 753-4559

Berkeley Mills Furniture
1704 Paseo de Peralta
Santa Fe, New Mexico 87501
(505) 982-4584

L.D. Burke III
1516 Pacheco Street
Santa Fe, New Mexico 87501
(505) 986-1866

Cassandra Lohr Design
    International, Inc.
P.O. Box 4611
Aspen, Colorado 81612
(970) 925-4799

Christopher Woolam Studio
P.O. Box 246
Arroyo Seco, New Mexico 87514
(505) 776-1851

Diane Cole
Rustic Furniture
10 Cloninger Lane
Bozeman, Montana 59715
(406) 586-3746

Covert Workshops
Cody, Wyoming

Cowboy Classics
Tom and Maril Bice
364 Main Street
Longmont, Colorado 80501
(303) 776-3394

Doolings of Santa Fe
525 Airport Road
Santa Fe, New Mexico 87501
(505) 471-5956

The Drawknife
99 West Highway 33
Tetonia, Idaho 83452
(208) 456-2560

Jerry England
Lure of the Dim Trails
22647 Ventura Boulevard
Woodland Hills, California 91364
(818) 702-0538

Fighting Bear Antiques
Terry and Sandy Winchell
P.O. Box 3812
Jackson, Wyoming 83001
(307) 733-2669

Ray Fisher
3 Amistad Place
Santa Fe, New Mexico 87501
(505) 466-8949

Roy Fisk
Lone Wolf Western Furnishings
Star Route Box 61
Jackson, Wyoming 83001
(307) 733-2822

Greg Flores
120 Bent Street
P.O. Box 2801
Taos, New Mexico 87571
(505) 758-9516

Frank Long & Company
8189 Huffine Lane
Bozeman, Montana 59715
(406) 587-5255

Jake Lemon
P.O. Box 2404
Sun Valley, Idaho 83353
(208) 788-3004

Livingston Furniture Design
17 West Fifth Avenue
Hutchinson, Kansas 67504
(316) 662-2781

Lupine Log Arts
13750 Kelly Canyon
Bozeman, Montana 59715
(406) 587-0672

J. Matt Madsen
P.O. Box 187
Orick, California 95555
(707) 488-3795

Teddy and Milo Marks
P.O. Box 208
Meridian, Texas 76665
(817) 435-2173

Jeremy Morrelli
Morrelli Corporation
540 South Guadalupe
Santa Fe, New Mexico 87501
(800) 739-6886

New West Furniture Company
J. Mike Patrick
2811 Bighorn Avenue
Cody, Wyoming 82414
(307) 587-2839

Joe and Paige Paisley
Paisley Products
1506 Shepard Place
Cody, Wyoming 82414
(307) 587-5477

Bruce Peterson
c/o Kent Galleries
130 Lincoln Avenue
Santa Fe, New Mexico 87501
(505) 988-1001

Rustic Ranch Furnishings
P.O. Box 1237
Terrell, Texas 75160
(214) 524-8894

Chris Sandoval
Artisans of the Desert
1625 Fourth Street NW
Albuquerque, New Mexico 87102
(505) 247-9725

Monte G. Scholten
2222 East Thomas Road
Phoenix, Arizona 85016
(602) 954-6271

Ken Siggins
Triangle Z Ranch
P.O. Box 995
Cody, Wyoming 82414
(307) 587-3901

Sombraje/Hillary Riggs
544 South Guadalupe
Santa Fe, New Mexico 87501
(505) 988-5567

Sweetwater Ranch
P.O. Box 398
Cody, Wyoming 82414
(307) 527-4044

Bob Waterman
P.O. Box 316
Basalt, Colorado 81621
(303) 927-4064

Wild West Furniture
Dick Kaplan
P.O. Box 3010
Apache Junction, Arizona 85278
(602) 963-4244

Willow Run Woodworking
2330 Amsterdam Road
Belgrade, Montana 59714
(406) 388-6848

HISTORICAL CENTERS/HOMES:

Buffalo Bill Historical Center
P.O. Box 1000
Cody, Wyoming 82414
(307) 587-4771

Fechin Institute
P.O. Box 832
Taos, New Mexico 87571
(505) 758-1710

Gamble House
4 Westmoreland Place
Pasadena, California 91103
(818) 793-3334

National Cowboy Hall of Fame
1700 NE 63rd Street
Oklahoma City, Oklahoma 73111
(405) 478-2250

TILE, HARDWARE, METALWORK, AND LEATHERWORK:

Tony Alvis
Wilderness Iron
6855 Vista del Rincon
Ventura, California 93001
(805) 648-2113

Gary Blank
Route 14, P.O. Box 317 GB
Santa Fe, New Mexico 87505
(505) 473-1115

Bert and Judy Hopple
P.O. Box 184
Wapiti, Wyoming 82450
(307) 527-7861

Karl Hipp Designs
131 Beaver Lane
Redstone, Colorado 81623
(303) 963-3755

Mexican Tile Company
2222 East Thomas Road
Phoenix, Arizona 85016
(602) 954-6271

John Mortensen
Rainbow Trail Collection
P.O. Box 746
Wilson, Wyoming 83014
(307) 733-1519

Pat Olson
P.O. Box 880767
Steamboat Springs, Colorado 80488
(303) 879-8377

Southwest Spanish Craftsmen
328 South Guadalupe
Santa Fe, New Mexico 87501
(505) 982-1767

Christopher Thomson
P.O. Box 578
Ribera, New Mexico
(505) 521-2645

True West Designs
21800 SE Highway 224
Clackamas, Oregon 97015
(503) 658-8753

WEAVINGS:

Carl Chew
7023 14th Avenue
Seattle, Washington 98115
(800) 644-6246
(206) 527-0797